T0262731

MUSEUM BUMS

MUSEUM BUMS

A Cheeky Look at Butts in Art

Mark Small and Jack Shoulder

CHRONICLE BOOKS
SAN FRANCISCO

Library of Congress Cataloging-in-Publication Data
Names: Shoulder, Jack, author. | Small, Mark (Mark A.), author.
Title: Museum bums : a cheeky look at butts in art / Jack Shoulder & Mark Small.
Description: San Francisco : Chronicle Books, 2023.
Identifiers: LCCN 2023007059 | ISBN 9781797218502 (hardcover)
Subjects: LCSH: Buttocks in art. | Art and society.
Classification: LCC N8217.B88 S56 2023 | DDC 704.9/42—dc23/eng/20230322
LC record available at https://lccn.loc.gov/2023007059

Manufactured in China.

MIX
Paper from responsible sources
FSC™ C169962

Design by Maggie Edelman.

10 9 8 7 6 5 4 3

Chronicle books and gifts are available at special quantity discounts to corporations, professional associations, literacy programs, and other organizations. For details and discount information, please contact our premiums department at corporatesales@chroniclebooks.com or at 1-800-759-0190.

Chronicle Books LLC
680 Second Street
San Francisco, California 94107
www.chroniclebooks.com

To those who have helped us see culture differently,
and to our teachers, friends, and family.

CONTENTS

INTRODUCTION

We all have bums. It's one of the things that unites us all. Butts can be all sorts of things—funny, silly, functional, scandalous, fleshy, and sexy—and we're here to celebrate the bottom in all its glory.

If you've been in a museum since 2016, you may have spotted us sneaking photos of statues' bums, giggling, and counting the bums on display. You may have seen us taking notes as to precisely why this particular painting has got so many bums (see pages 71–74 for Hieronymus Bosch's bonkers bum-filled paintings) or pondering what the artist is trying to communicate by sculpting this bottom just so. We've honed our museum bum-spotting senses to a fine point, and now we are ready to share our findings with the world.

Even though visiting museums and scouring them for their best butts is what we do for fun in our spare time, in real life we are actually serious heritage professionals, working locally and nationally in cultural venues and heritage sites in the UK.

Through our endeavours, we've noticed butts have been a huge part of art since the first humans started making and creating. The earliest known figures of people put the "donk" in "ba-donkadonk" (see pages 20–23), and the earliest known chat-up line in the earliest recorded literature was "Hi, nice ass" (or words to that effect; you'll have to bone up on your ancient Egyptian to get the real nuance). In fact, by paying attention to the bottom line, we can see how artists have developed their skills and their knowledge of musculature, from the simple lines of ancient Egyptian art, to the perfect proportions of the classical world, to the fleshy realism of later artists.

And so we decided to write this book all about the long-standing impact of the bum, right through to present-day art. We'll be looking at some familiar pieces of art from a whole new angle (see the statue of David on page 43) and thinking about them in a whole new way.

Art with a capital *A* can be intimidating, but we're here to offer a cheeky view of what's on display in the hallowed halls of museums and cultural spaces all over the world. By sharing our unique point of view, we want to help you see things from a different perspective and see Art in a whole new way.

In these pages we've got boys' bums, girls' bums, other people's bums, devilishly sexy bums, Olympian callipygia, human-shaped bums on monsters, and things that aren't bums at all but are if you concentrate hard enough.

We also put a big old rainbow spotlight on queer bums and explore how LGBTQIA+ artists have depicted the human form.

As well as admiring these beautiful bottoms, we'll also be asking the big questions, like . . .

- Are we *supposed* to be seeing these bottoms?
- Who was looking at them in the first place and what does that say about the object?

- Have you noticed that the vast majority of bodies represented in museums are male, white, muscly, a narrow definition of pretty, and cisgender? If you haven't, you will now!

We start by looking at the bums, then asking *why* this bum is here in this museum, or gallery, or archive, or library, or another cultural space, and thinking about what that bum is trying to tell us. We'll explore how even though what's on the walls and in collections often shows physical perfection, in real life, people exist in a variety of shapes and sizes; that people of colour are everywhere, and always have been despite what museums and galleries present through their displays; that "pretty" isn't defined by long-dead white men; and that trans people, queer people, and gender nonconforming people have always existed, are valid, and by the gods they deserve to see themselves celebrated alongside the rest of humanity in museums. We'll be covering all of this through the medium of butts.

We'll make you laugh, we'll make you think, and we'll help you realise that sometimes, to really get to know something, you need to look at it from the backside.

So, sit comfortably, enjoy, and get ready for some bums.

To help you on your journey through time, space, art, and the best bottoms museums have to offer, here are some words you might like to know before embarking:

bum: that thing you sit on, very nice to look at. In America it's a butt or a fanny, or an ass.

callipygian: having well-shaped buttocks (*kallos* is Greek for beauty, and *puge* is Greek for buttocks).

contrapposto: (Italian for "opposite") a term specific to statues. If you shift your weight to one leg and raise that hip, you tense one bumcheek and relax the other. That's contrapposto! In the Western world, the contrapposto stance started appearing in the fifth century BCE, when the Greeks felt like being radically different to earlier *kouros* and ancient Egyptian statue forms. It looks good, right?

The bums presented in the pages that follow were lovingly curated from our adventures. It's certainly not an exhaustive list of every bottom in every museum, so we hope this book inspires you to hunt for more bums in the museums near you or to seek them out in your travels.

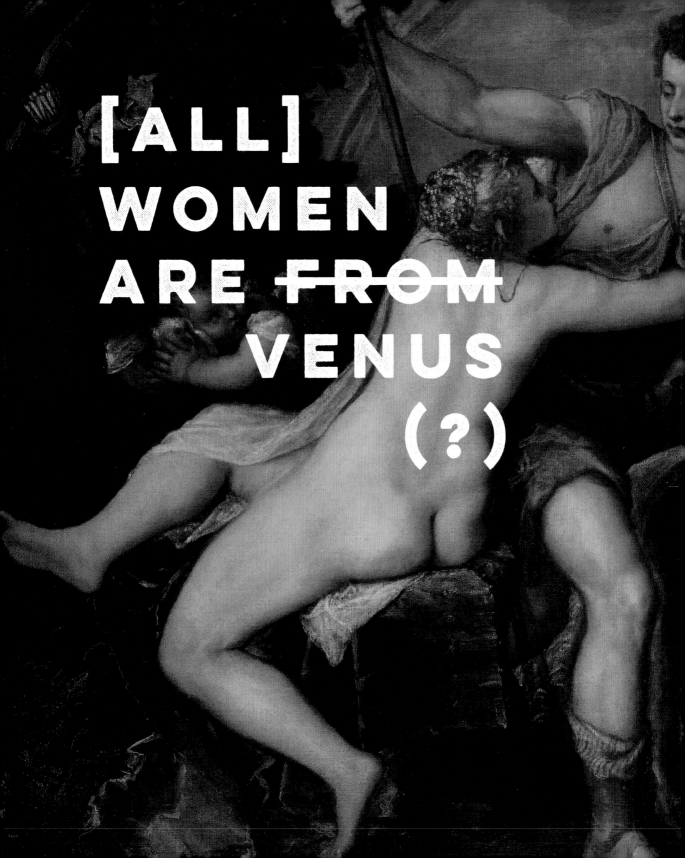

[ALL]
WOMEN
ARE ~~FROM~~
VENUS
(?)

Here's Titian's 1550s Venus attempting to stop Adonis from leaving her to go hunting, as she was worried he'd get killed (spoiler: he got killed). Moral of this story? Hunting is bad, cuddles with Venus are good!

You can see this one at the Metropolitan Museum of Art in New York.

Imagine you're in a museum. The galleries echo with your footsteps, and you come to a stop in front of a nude female figure. No matter which museum you're in, there's a very good chance you are standing in front of (or behind) a version of Venus. You may have heard of Venus: she's the Roman goddess in charge of love, desire, and fertility. If there's a sex scandal in classical mythology, it'll either be Venus or Zeus at the centre of it all (see more on Zeus in "Gods and Monsters," page 28). Venus is probably most familiar to us as the one without any arms (see *Venus de Milo* on page 15), but she's also the one who famously has the pert, pretty, proportional bottom (see *Venus Callipyge* on pages 16–17).

Across Europe, prehistoric stuff, stuff that's thousands of years older than the perfect symmetrical and proportional classical Venuses, keeps getting dug up. Some of this stuff is the only surviving trace of those pre-written-record civilizations. Archaeologists, curators, and other people involved in giving names to old stuff have decided to call all unidentified ancient female figures and depictions "Venus." The squat, sturdy, fat frames of these Stone Age Venuses (check out *Venus of Willendorf* on page 19) with their emphasis on the breasts, buttocks, and bellies are a world away from the leggy "perfect" proportions prescribed by Praxiteles and other ancient Greek artists or the strawberry-blonde Botticelli beauties bestriding bivalves. So how are they the same deity? *Are* they the same deity?

But we're getting ahead of ourselves. Let's get back to the bright white, classically beautiful, proportionally perfect Aphrodite and Venus of the ancient Greeks and Romans.

This chapter takes you on a journey through depictions of beauty; symmetry being the "sexiest" view; Victorian men policing women's bodies and what they had decided fertility looks like; and how suffragettes responded to the injustice of having women's bums on display in galleries to be gawked at by guys. The prehistoric Venus is going to tell us about fat, powerful women; the practicalities of fertility; how this comes across in the statues; and how depictions of Venus have shaped what "sexy" has meant over the last 29,000 years.

Venus was known by the Greeks as Aphrodite ("frothy-lady," for the literally minded amongst you, as she was born fully formed from seafoam). Embodying the epitome of beauty, ancient artists (many of them male) depicted her with what they had decided were perfect proportions. This is not just a woman, this is a goddess, and she's the first representation of love, beauty, and all that comes with it to be encapsulated into a human figure in the Western tradition.

What we're saying is, Venus wouldn't look like the classical girl next door. (Although . . . Praxiteles was an ancient Greek artist who modelled his *Aphrodite of Knidos* statue after his mistress, possibly a famous courtesan called Phryne. See his efforts at charming a lady on page 17. So in that *very* specific case, Venus really did look like Praxiteles's girlfriend, who must have been someone's neighbour, and therefore quite literally the classical girl next door.)

From the moment Venus burst forth from her bubbles she was the perfect excuse for artists to depict the female form in all its glory. Classical artists saw little need for their Venuses to cover up.

Their sexy, symmetrical statues were designed to adorn temples; their bright, bold, brash hues were a world away from the stark white marble we see today in museums. The *Aphrodite of Knidos*, with her contrapposto pose emphasizing her curves, and as one ancient Greek writer says, "wearing only a smile," was purchased by Knidos to bring fame and fortune to the town. There are legends that the statue was so beautiful that Aphrodite herself paid a visit.

As you can see, Praxiteles's *Aphrodite of Knidos* is far from flaunting her features (not that that gives men any license to impose themselves on women, goddesses or otherwise), though she's demurely depicted disrobed but dignified, reaching for her towel. If you know your mythology, you'll know it never ends well for the mortal who steals a glimpse (or more) of an unsuspecting goddess. Blindness, transfiguration, and death usually befall those who incur divine wrath.

As with so many things that are wrong with the world, the policing of women's bodies and the impact that had on museums can be traced back to Victorian men. It's no coincidence that the rise of strict Victorian rules about what beautiful women were supposed to look like (and not look like) mirrored the opening of museums displaying classical statues to a more general public. The neoclassical echoed the classical in art and architecture, but also in standards of beauty, and these were imposed on women. In the Victorian era, the classical Venuses were back in fashion, nude, and exhibited for male scholars and aesthetes (and a small number of female scholars and aesthetes; we're not dealing in absolutes here), but under male control. Men who ran museums decided that these women, who were curvy but not too curvy; beautiful but demure; strong, but quite literally created and owned by men, were the blueprint for a goddess in human form. And this was all translated back onto the living and breathing women of the Victorian age, and we're still seeing the repercussions in the twenty-first century.

When we look at all these depictions of Venus, we should think, "Are we being invited to look at her?" and more importantly, "Who is inviting us?" If the answers are "Yes" and "My girl, V," then by all means admire them. If the answers are anything else, beware the wrath of one of the scariest and most vengeful gods in the pantheon!

Look at the *Rokeby Venus* (see page 18); she's reclining with her back to you. She's gazing into her mirror, but you can't directly see her face (because how can you paint perfection?). It's all very dreamy and hazy, with luxurious, velvety fabrics adding a luxurious, velvety quality to the picture. The only fleshy, three-dimensional detailed part of the painting is Venus's bottom. The viewers are drawn to the curve of her hip and muscle. Is Venus allowing us to admire her? Or is Cupid holding the mirror revealing to his mother who the voyeurs are? Are you invading Venus's privacy?

Men gazing upon Venus uninvited was one of the factors that led to a violent attack on this painting in the National Gallery in London. In 1914, the *Rokeby*

Venus (a rare example of a nude Venus painted by Spanish artist Velázquez) was chopped, hacked, and slashed at least five times with a knife. The attacker was not a lovesick male worshipper but an angry woman: Mary Richardson. Richardson was a suffragette (and later a follower of fascist Oswald Mosely) who became known as "Slasher Mary."

Richardson was protesting the arrest of Emmeline Pankhurst, a leader in the British women's suffrage movement. She told the press that she "tried to destroy the picture of the most beautiful woman in mythological history as a protest against the Government for destroying Mrs. Pankhurst, who is the most beautiful character in modern history," and that she objected to "the way men visitors gaped at it all day long." Now we are all for supporting the rights of women, but not by a) attacking other women, or b) supporting fascism, or c) stepping up to the Divine Miss V.

Luckily for all of us, the painting was restored.

Undoubtedly there's something thrilling about laying eyes on a goddess, but Venus's nudity is not just tied to the erotic. It can mean all sorts of things:

1. New life: When we see her on her clam in Botticelli's *The Birth of Venus* (which unfortunately doesn't feature her bum!), art historians think it suggests new life, as she's just been created.
2. Sex: Venus is about love and sex. Alongside being connected with new life, she's also responsible for the urge that sets these things in motion, so the cycle of life continues.
3. Procreation: This aspect of her godliness

is clearest when we look at the Roman Venus, who was known as Venus Genetrix, or Venus the Mother, because she was the mother of Aeneas, one of the mythical founders of Rome. As a mother she's not often seen nude, so there aren't too many Venus Genetrix museum bums. Mythologically speaking, Venus had other children, like Eros, Hermaphrodite, and the Graces, whose glorious godlike glutes make an appearance in "Gods and Monsters" on page 28.

So how on earth did we get to these silky-smooth marble Aphrodites from the rough-hewn, sometimes barely decipherable bootylicious "Venuses" of thousands of years before?

Venus is a symbol of fertility, and all evidence points to the understanding that these prehistoric female figurines, literally some of the earliest works of art ever created, like *Venus of Willendorf* (see page 19), were worshipped female symbols. They have exaggerated feminine features (we're including lady bums here as feminine features), so they probably had something to do with fertility.

There are a few things to take away from this:

1. Yay! Women are powerful and important.
2. Yay! Fatness is powerful and important.
3. Yay! People throughout history (including today) are valuing Venus as an important member of the ultra-pantheon of gods.
4. Boo! Venus is one female figure from one belief system, and you've decided that instead of giving more than one woman power, you're just going to call any unidentified woman from the whole of Europe, from the whole of time "Venus," because that's easier for your typologies than accepting that prehistoric cultures across Europe had nothing to do with the classical pantheon and that all women are powerful, not just that one lady who clambered out of a clam shell! For Venus's sake!

There is another issue. Venus of the classical pantheon, the one who's "at her toilette" in the *Rokeby Venus* (see page 18) is . . . statuesque. She's Rubenesque. She's got swerves and curves. But the prehistoric "Venuses," like *Venus of Lespugue* (see page 20) and *Venus of Dolní Vestonice* (see page 20), take swerves and curves to another level. They are "chunky yet funky," to quote drag performer Latrice Royale. They are Venus at her most essential, and at her most universal.

This means that there's a cognitive misstep between the classical Venus—who *is* a fertility goddess but whose fertility has been portrayed mostly by men, with a (skinnier) modern-era understanding of fertility and beauty—and somehow applying that same name to the bountiful, bootiful fertility goddesses we're digging up from 25,000 years ago.

We guess this can be summed up by saying that classical Venus's fertility is manifested through what a small section of male classical sculptors would see as sexy. (And the resonance of classical imagery throughout the next three millennia means that *that* understanding of sexiness plays a large part in what *we* see as sexy.)

Conversely, the prehistoric "Venus's" fertility is manifested through the practicalities of what a fertile woman's body does. For those female figures, fertility is more practical than cosmetic. It isn't (necessarily) "she's hot," it's "my big boobs are giving me a backache." We're still thinking about ideal proportions, but in a practical rather than an aesthetic way. So the ancient "Venuses" are showing fertility not as something desirable to the male gaze (possibly because they weren't made by or for men, and the story they're telling certainly isn't male-centric). Boobs = breastfeeding, vulvas = procreation, big butt = big childbearing hips and having

a better chance of surviving the abject terror of childbirth.

Don't get us wrong. We are certainly not saying that the prehistoric figurines are not sexy. We're saying that fertility isn't a one-circle Venn diagram with male desire at its centre. And the prehistoric folks understood that!

Now that you can put Venus (or "Venus") in context, go have a look at the rest of the chapter of our favourite goddess and her bootiful bum.

When you plan to have a productive Saturday but instead you get out of the shower and sit on the bed for five hours playing Sudoku on your phone.

The Louvre's *Venus de Milo* is one of the most famous classical statues ever. She's appeared in everything from Disney's *Hercules* to Duke Ellington's "Chocolate Shake," including the line "Venus de Milo had charms; she gave the Greeks quite a break. Now that poor gal is minus her arms, from doin' the Chocolate Shake." Divine.

This photo of female admirers checking out *Venus Callipyge* at the National Archaeological Museum of Naples in 1952, by David Seymour, makes us so happy. You can almost feel the sapphic awakenings happening behind some of those eyes! (See page 11 for the full story.)

Aphrodite of Knidos is said to be the most beautiful statue from the ancient world. Made to adorn the temple to the goddess, the statue drew visitors and worshippers from all over. According to legend, there was a certain male worshipper who snuck into the temple after hours in an attempt to make love to the statue. After waking from his post-coital nap, he realised that he had stained the statue. Overcome with shame, he threw himself into the sea. The original *Aphrodite of Knidos* has been lost to us, but copies, approximations, and translations of the statue can be found in museums all over the world.

Venus Callipyge literally translates as "Venus with the beautiful bum." You can see why Ms. V gets her own chapter, right?

To us it looks like she's giving "when you've lost the fight with the bedsheet but decide to style it out" vibes. Can relate.

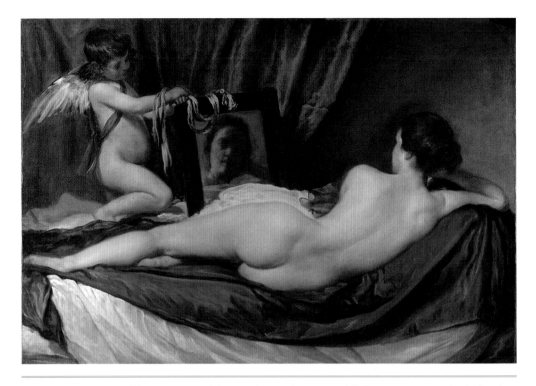

Diego Velázquez's *Venus del espejo* (*Venus of the Mirror*) at London's National Gallery is a rare example of a female nude by Velázquez and pretty much unique as a Spanish depiction of Venus from this era, but that's not the only reason she's noteworthy . . . *makes the *Psycho* violin screeches and a knifey stabbing motion*

 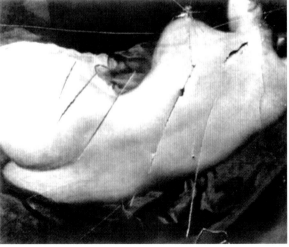

The suffragette Mary Richardson slashed the *Rokeby Venus* with a kitchen knife as a protest (see page 13 for the full story).

Stop, wait, no! Don't put the Gonnersdorf Venus in your loafers! She is not a shoehorn!

Well . . . anything can be a shoehorn with enough patience and deep breaths, but the Gonnersdorf Venus is not *primarily* a shoehorn. Don't worry, even the experts haven't realised her full potential.

She is between 11,000 and 15,000 years old and she's possibly made from mammoth ivory, so put her down gently!

She's big, she's bountiful, she's beautiful! <3

The *Venus of Willendorf* is at the Natural History Museum in Vienna. She's only 11 cm tall but she packs a punch, doesn't she? She was discovered in 1908 as part of an excavation of a palaeolithic site in Austria, and they reckon she's more than 20,000 years old.

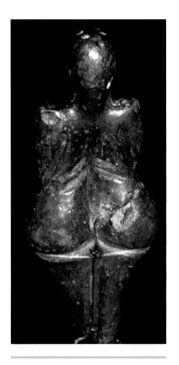

This curvy lady is the *Venus of Dolní Věstonice*, so called because she was excavated at Dolní Věstonice (surprise!) in the Czech Republic. She's around 29,000 years old.

Dang, V of L!

This bodacious babe, the *Venus of Lespugue*, is made from mammoth ivory and was found in the Grotte des Rideaux (in Lespugue, France). She currently lives in the Musée de l'Homme in Paris.

This replica was made to show how the *Venus of Lespugue* might have looked when freshly sculpted.

Unlike Botticelli's famous version of the *Birth of Venus*, Marco Dente's etched engraving here shows Venus inventing surfing. You can tell it's good art because there are derpy fish . . . *nods sagely*

Dente's engraving dates from c. 1516 and beautifully encapsulates Venus's origin story of being born of sea spray and blown by the windy god Zephyrus to the island of Cyprus.

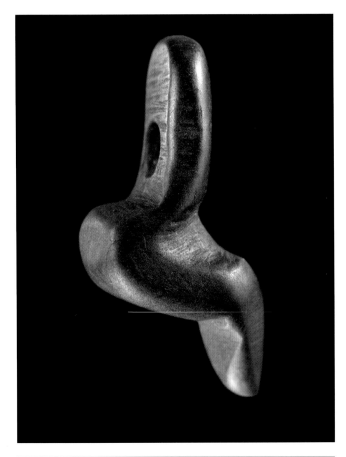

With banana bread, house plants, and cross-stitch back in style, it was only inevitable that macramé bras, last seen in Kostenki, Russia, in 18000 BCE, would make a comeback.

This is the *Kostenki Venus*, now residing in the Hermitage Museum, and the "macramé bra" is actually thought to be an early depiction of a bandeau.

This Venus also acts as a handy carabiner for when you need to rapel out of the museum at the end of the art heist.

She could hold her own in any modern gallery or avant-garde sculpture park, but actually the *Venus de Monruz* is a good 11,000 years old. She was dug up in 1991 when workers constructed a motorway in Switzerland.

We've all seen this stance. Mum/Gran/Titi is not mad, she's just disappointed. We'd better apologise and look like we mean it, quick.

This is a Cycladic marble figure from about 4,000 to 4,500 years ago from Southern Europe, and now she lives in the Met in New York (but we'd love her on our shelf to remind us to phone those maternal figures in our lives more often).

Hold the bums in this image right up close to your eyes, closer, bit closer, go on, it's fine, no one's laughing at you in the library. OK, now look at all those tiny dots like pixels, except each one was etched to make a print. Can you imagine how many hours Angelo Bertini spent staring at Venus and Mars's arses to get this engraving right?

This is an engraving by Angelo Bertini, after a drawing by Giovanni Tognolli, after a sculpture by Antonio Canova. That's a lot of people who've spent a hell of a lot of time creating and recreating these beautiful bums for us. Aren't we lucky? These days this print is part of the collections at the Rijksmuseum in Amsterdam.

VENERE E MARTE

A Sua Altezza Reale

Giorgio Federico Augusto Principe di Galles

Reggente della Gran Brettagna &c. &c. &c. &c.

Gruppo in marmo, essendo al vero, simboleggiante la Guerra, e la Pace, appartenente alla R.A.S.

Antonio Canova

VENERE

A Sua Altezza I.R. Madama Elisa
Principessa di Lucca e di Piombino
Gran Duchessa di Toscana

Antonio Canova P.D.D.

Ocupado! When your goddamn roommate forgets to goddamn knock on the goddamn bathroom door for the goddamn millionth time!!

Master sculptor Antonio Canova really knocked it out of the park with this one. This one's another etching of a drawing of a statue by Canova. In the Rijksmuseum, Amsterdam.

Dorme Clori: coll arpa Amor la desta:
Sorge sul fianco, e ad ascoltar s' arresta.

"Mum! Mum! Mum! Mum! Mum! Mum! Look! Mum! Mum! Look! Mum! Look what I can do! Mum! You're not looking! Mum! Mum! Look Mum! Look!"

Back View of Venus Reclining Accompanied by Cupid with a Harp, an etching by Domenico Marchetti (1817), after a sketch by Giovanni Tognolli, after a sculpture by Canova.

Shall I do all the laundry again, then? Even deities can't escape chores.

Michelangelo Pistoletto's *Venus of the Rags* has been recreated by the artist a number of times, including one with a gold goddess and one in 1980 in San Francisco with a live model.

GODS
AND
MONSTERS

In many cultures gods represent the human-shaped embodiment of an abstract concept, like love; or the personification of something that's fundamentally important, like the sea. In depicting their gods, humans present them as an ideal physical specimen, even when they represent something bad, like war or death. This is particularly true for the gods worshipped by the Greeks and Romans. Greek artists were trained to use ideal proportions and present perfection. Roman artists were trained to copy the Greeks. Throughout the centuries, artists have often looked back to this perfect moment in art history for guidance and inspiration.

By focusing only on producing "perfection," these artists don't show us what the human bodies can look like and they reveal the biases and phobias of their contemporary societies. Through idealising the muscular youth and the soft curves of the goddess, ancient sculptors aren't even showing us the full range of bodies that exist on Olympus. Hephaestus, the blacksmith god (see *Vulcan* on page 30; Vulcan was what the Romans called Hephaestus), is described as being disabled, usually "lame," by poets, but in his rare depictions, his body is still the muscular ideal.

A different example from a different era displays the same issue: brand-new statues in the ancient world were covered in kitsch, brash, in-your-face, colourful decoration. Being buried underground, or underwater (see Antikythera statue, page 146), or being left to the elements for

thousands of years meant these gaudy, colourful, and diverse statues ended up losing most of their decoration, including skin tone, before they were rediscovered in the modern age. In fact, as late as the 1930s, when the British Museum found hints and traces of colour on the Parthenon Marbles, the museum "polished" off the pigment because it didn't fit with how they wanted to view the past. "Polishing" may be too gentle a word here; scrubbed off with a wire brush is much closer to the truth of the matter. This meant that the statues that the people were elevating to the highest of High Art were not just white, they were blindingly, brilliantly white. Any trace of understanding that anyone not white could have existed in a non-enslaved or exotic-and-therefore-not-civilised way in the classical world was scrubbed away. The "new" art created in the neoclassical mode with those classical statues as their inspiration almost ubiquitously featured white skin.

Speaking of removing colour, we need to talk about Andromeda. Have a look at the pictures by Edward Burne-Jones on this chapter's title page. She looks like every other princess in peril, complete with long auburn hair and an alabaster back. This is what a princess looks like, right? Well, not quite. According to Ovid, a Roman poet who left us a treasure trove of Greek and Roman myths, Perseus travels over Libya to reach Ethiopia to rescue monster-bait Andromeda, who is chained to a rock, waiting to be feasted on

There was me, ready to start lathering up and this thing climbed right out of the plughole!
Sir Edward Burne-Jones's *The Perseus Series: Doom Fulfilled*, 1900, held by Birmingham Museums Trust.

Vulcan is the blacksmith god, whom the Greeks called Hephaestus. His godly smithing, crafting arms, and armour for other gods and their favourite heroes have given him an impressive upper body. In some traditions, Vulcan is lame because he was thrown from Mount Olympus as he tried to intervene in a fight between Zeus and Hera, and fell for nine days. In other traditions, he was born with mobility issues. This statue is the largest cast-iron statue in the world. It was created as Birmingham's entry for the Louisiana Purchase Exposition (1904 St. Louis World's Fair) in St. Louis, Missouri. The godly subject and the material chosen reflect Birmingham's iron and steel industrial history.

by a monstrous beast. Why is she in this position? Because her mother, Cassiopeia, boasted about how beautiful she was. Not her daughter, herself. This insulted some dryads, who asked Poseidon for a spot of fatherly vengeance. Which brings us to the current situation, with Andromeda chained to a rock, suddenly given a deus ex machina in the form of Perseus swooping in to save the day using Medusa's granite-glare to stop the sea monster in its tracks (see page 32).

Here's why this is important: Andromeda was the princess of Ethiopia (which at that point wasn't necessarily the modern country of Ethiopia, but it was definitely in Africa). How easy would it have been to depict Princess Andromeda, Princess of Ethiopia, who, like her mother, was also a renowned beauty (and whose name literally translates to "I protect, I rule over men"), as a strong, powerful, regal, and wronged Black woman? Although ancient black figure vases depicted her as white, they depicted Perseus with black skin. This is because skin colouring was coded according to gender; men had dark skin from being outside and women had to deal with inside activities. With such a clear indication of where Andromeda was from, auburn hair and an alabaster complexion feel very out of place for an East African princess.

There has been a long history, intentional or not, of whitewashing the world of the ancient Mediterranean and its encounters with the people of Africa. Sir EB-J created his interpretation of Percy and Andy in 1876. He studied at Oxford, which tells us he was an intelligent chap, so he could have easily connected the dots with Andromeda, should he have put his mind to it. However, he allegedly had a "revolt from fact," so maybe he didn't pay too much attention to the details of things and merely painted his own ideal of beauty rather than thinking, "What would Andromeda, famed for her beauty, have looked like?"

This idealisation and perfection are issues even when constructing the monsters. Some artists made statues that have us feeling a bit confused. Why *is* that monster so hunky? (See the *Minotaur* on page 57.) Encountering both gods and monsters should inspire some flavour of fear, either awe or argh! Both also teach us lessons. The word *monster* has the same root as *demonstrate*; these creatures show us something: the minotaur might be a representation of the animal urges we keep buried deep inside us, sirens show us how dangerous it can be to only follow our

passions, and gorgons . . . gorgons reflect all kinds of things back to us. Artists have often used monstrosity to portray those out-of-control, animalistic urges like lust and hunger that we oh-so-often try to repress.

We can feel sorry for monsters, too. Some of them inspire pity and show us our humanity. Are they really that monstrous, or are they victims of terrible circumstances?

We decided right at the start that *Museum Bums* was going to set a boundary at sharing human and human-ish-shaped bums. This means cheeky charming fauns (see Edward Burne-Jones's *Pan and Psyche*, page 34), suspiciously sexy minotaurs, and capering callipygian satyrs (see page 41) get a look in, but we don't have to trawl through natural history collections, deciding if beetle carapaces count as bums. But what about centaurs? That depends on which half is the horse. And see Sarah Hingley's *Fishbutt Fandango* on page 52 to see what you get when you're not specific enough in your wish for a merperson!

A note: we are drawing heavily from the stories told in ancient Greece and Rome. We'd love to research more into the gods and monsters of other cultures, but because there is an unfair weighting of classical, European history over other periods, styles, and geographical areas, it's harder to explore examples from other cultures in as much depth. Many museums started as the personal collections of rich men in the eighteenth and nineteenth centuries, who'd pillaged their ways around their Grand Tours of Hellenic Europe and North Africa, before endowing their collection "to the people." (There's a lot to unpack here and none of it is fun and light-hearted. If you want to read more about this instead of bums, have a read of *The Brutish Museums* by Professor Dan Hicks, and *Culture Is Bad for You* by Orion Brook, Dave O'Brien, and Mark Taylor.)

Fortunately, museums are chock-full of bottom-heavy representations from mythology gleefully telling stories of gods behaving badly. It would take several books to fully detail all the terrible, awful things Zeus has done: kidnapping Ganymede, impersonating Alcmene's husband, impersonating Artemis to get close to one of her followers, turning Io into a cow to avoid the wrath of his wife Hera. The other Greek gods were hardly better, so bumping into the gods is bad news for mortals.

And then there's Medusa. Poor Medusa. She was one of Athena's priestesses and served the goddess in her temple. According to Ovid, Poseidon, the god of the sea, desires Medusa and brutally assaults her while she is attending to her duties. She cries out to Athena for help. Rather than helping her poor priestess, Athena curses her with scaly skin, serpentine locks, and a petrifying stare. Her alleged crime? Defiling the temple. Poseidon, on the other hand, swims away scot-free.

There is only a very thin line separating the divine from the demonic.

It is unusual for Medusa's body to be represented in art. Her power was in her eyes, which has led to artists focusing on her head. To add insult to injury, where her body is present, it is usually discarded in a heap on the floor. Medusa has gone from being a powerful woman to having

others exploiting her petrifying glare. It's not uncommon to see Perseus holding her head triumphantly aloft (see page 42). His heroic pose is designed to show strength radiating from every muscle (even his bum). By holding Medusa aloft, the artist is signalling to us that we should be looking up at Percy, figuratively and literally, from all angles. In enabling us to admire this statue from behind as well, the artist is letting us interact with the legend of Perseus and Medusa without joining them in stony stillness.

There is *some* #JusticeForMedusa as her head-based depictions quickly shed her monstrous connotations. Technically called *gorgoneion*, they soon started sitting atop buildings, breastplates, and tombstones to act as a guardian and ward off evil. She's even the face of Versace now. Good for her.

Medusa's story sees her transition from maiden to monster, but there are other beings whose story runs in the opposite direction, from the scary to the sensual. Sirens are an interesting one to consider. They have transformed in the popular imagination from women with bird bodies, whose sensuality sits only in their songs, to sultry sea-dwelling seductresses, not unlike mermaids. Mermaids who, would you believe, have actual butts (see page 56). Museums are perfect places to ponder the age-old question that perplexed sailors since they started spending too long at sea: "Do mermaids have bums?" We're pleased to tell you the answer is "Yes!"

Sirens have come to represent what happens when we give in to temptation and follow our desires. We are dragged under the waves, crushed against ragged rocks, or torn apart and eaten (metaphorically, of course). Moving forward in time by about 1,900 years, we have some monster bums that are much more modern. The modern palette gives us a whole level of hell of monstrous depictions. Everything from the unsettling nightmares of Francis Bacon's part-human, part-blobs (see page 53) to Sarah Hingley's somehow adorable *Fishbutt Fandango* (see page 52).

That's monsters' butts taken care of. Now, what about the gods?

Believe it or not, some ancient gods weren't absolute garbage fires. If you've been to an exhibition on ancient Rome, you may have seen some rather fabulous statues of Antinous, Roman emperor Hadrian's boyfriend/partner/lover/favourite/cupbearer/#godbae. If you haven't, then here's a nice surprise for you! Emperor Hadrian (yes, the one who built the wall) had a wife as society expected, but the love of his life was a young man called Antinous. Some ally at the British Museum has very romantically put Antinous's and Hadrian's busts next to each other. Antinous was renowned for his unnatural beauty; no one could deny how pretty he was. His pouty lips and curly hair are particularly praised by art historians. After Antinous's mysterious death by drowning in the River Nile, Hadrian used his gods-given power as an emperor to deify Ant so that he could continue living forever.

Rome was fine with Hadrian having a boyfriend, but quite a few politically powerful men felt that making him a god was a bit much. Usually this kind of honour was meant solely for the emperors and their immediate family, so they may have had a point; alternatively, you could say that Hadrian raised the bar for romantic partners everywhere, and if your partner isn't treating you like an actual god, then are they really measuring up?

Now that you're all caught up, here's the best bit: Hadrian really pushed Antinous's cult and commissioned a lot of statues reflecting the radiant beauty of his lover. Even the Vatican has a statue of *Antinous Osiris* in their collections. Dearest Ant's bum is the very definition of *callipygian* ("beautiful buttocks"), at least according to all the statues (see page 35—*Antinous Farnese*—and you'll see why he turns our heads!). Since the Romans there have been many romantic resurgences of the cult of Antinous, with queer gentlemen professing their love for the handsome god through his many statuesque representations and using him as a secret code to help identify others who worship him too.

As you pay homage to the godly glutes and shrink in terror at the beastly backsides that grace the next chapter, consider: Which of the figures are *truly* monstrous?

Edward Burne-Jones's *Pan and Psyche* (c. 1872) in his distinctive pre-Raphaelite style shows yet another guy in Psyche's life treating her badly. No one needs to be told to worship their ex, just google *Cupid and Psyche*!

This one comes from Birmingham Museums Trust in the UK.

Look at this handsome young man. Can you blame Roman emperor Hadrian for falling head over heels in love? Nope, us either.

Antinous (lovingly known as "godbae" in these halls) was the deified youth famed for his beauty and for being the love of Hadrian's life; there are billions of statues of this beguiling gentleman and they all have fantastic bums.

This one's at the National Archaeological Museum of Naples.

When you jump into your fella's arms because you spot the spider scuttling across the floor.

Hercules and Antaeus are a popular pair for sculptures, and almost always feature a bum. Antaeus's magic strength came from contact with the ground, so clever Herc did the *Dirty Dancing* lift to defeat him en route to one of his labours.

There are many depictions of these two hugging, but this one's at the Rijksmuseum in Amsterdam.

Buckle in, this is a wild one. So Marsyas is a satyr who has superhuman musical abilities. He challenges Apollo to a music duel and whips the crowd into a frenzy with his jazz flute. Apollo goes for a different tack and plays lyre and sings so beautifully that the crowd is overcome with emotion. Having lost the riff-off, Apollo then skins Marsyas and makes a wineskin out of the hide. Scholars reckon there's something here about chastened love (Apollo) being greater and more worthy of a win than dirty, mucky, lustful rock 'n' roll (Marsyas). We think it's just Apollo being a monster while also being a god.

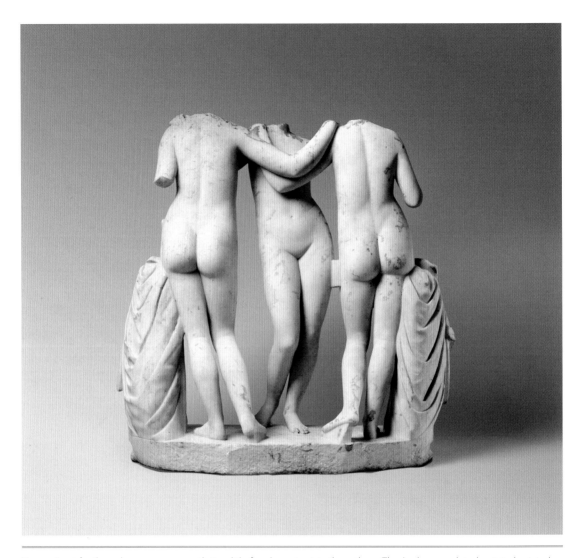

You can't get far through any museum worth its salt before bumping into these three. They've been sculpted, painted, minted, carved, etched, sketched, moulded, and printed more times than you can shake a stick at. They're a perennial favourite for artists because it's not just one nude lady but three!

  These three grace the halls of the Metropolitan Museum of Art in New York.

Paris and his peach? Oh wait, no, that's an apple "for the fairest."

Paris was a mortal prince who was given the unenviable task of telling three goddesses which of them was the most beautiful, via a golden, delicious apple.

Here's another engraving of a drawing of a statue from Rijksmuseum! This one's from 1785.

ALLA MAESTÀ DI GIVSEPPINA IMPERATRICE

Antonio   Canova D.D.D.

We imagine that working with the dead, like the god Pluto does, is probably a messy business—how else would you explain P-Dog here wearing his fabulous flowing cape the wrong way around? The chiaroscuro woodcut of Pluto surveying his kingdom was made by Hendrick Goltzius, 1588–1590.

RP-P-OB-38.487

What's better than a dog with one beautiful doggy face? Cerberus with three beautiful doggy faces <3. It's almost enough to distract you from Hercules's Herculean bum.

This very good boy (and Hercules) is at the Rijkmuseum.

Claude Michel, also known as Clodion, specialised in bacchic orgies. What a line to have on your résumé!

Well, specifically, he specialised in making little models of them. Like a little ceramic Warhammer but they all kiss. Awwwww.

Look at these two having a great time! You can catch them at the Met in New York.

Nymphs are essentially your high school Mean Girls, but in Greek myth. In five minutes' time, the hanger is going to set in when they realise Phoebe didn't pack the picnic.

Bouguereau's *Nymphaeum*, 1878, is at the Haggin Museum in California, USA.

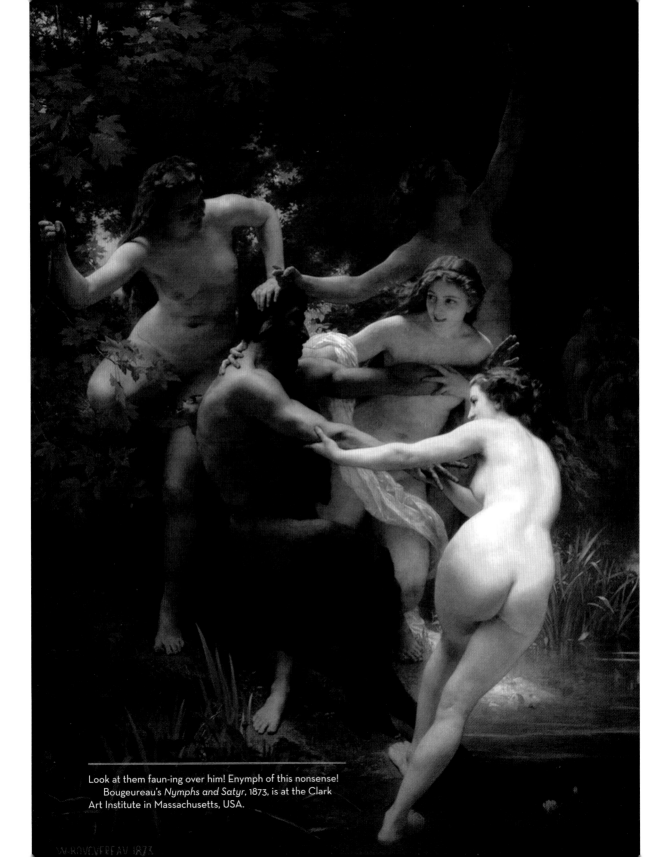

Look at them faun-ing over him! Enymph of this nonsense!
Bougeureau's *Nymphs and Satyr*, 1873, is at the Clark
Art Institute in Massachusetts, USA.

#JusticeForMedusa.

Aratus definitely captured Medusa's "I'm not having a good day" vibe here.

This is a page from *Leiden Aratea*, which is at Leiden University Library in the Netherlands.

#JusticeForMedusa.

Pert, peachy Perseus, posing proudly. Putz.

Canova's *Perseus* is one of the most viewed exhibits at the Metropolitan Museum of Art in New York and we love how it looks but also we have a deep distaste for Percy.

With their superhuman feats, heroes are often thought of as being godlike. In so many cases, heroes are the children of gods, making them somewhat godly themselves. David (above and to the right) is a hero who is well known to many from his exploits in the book of Samuel. He slays giants, is in an accomplished lyre player, and becomes a decent king. He's not the son of anyone special; he's a shepherd boy who has an extraordinary journey. Along the way, David falls in love with his companion, Jonathan. They share a bed, exchange embraces, and love each other in a way that is described as being marriage-like. But all too often they are described as "just friends." Michelangelo's towering hero is one of the most iconic artworks of all time. His work owes a lot to the classical depictions of gods and heroes, and over and over again Michelangelo's work prompts us to think about the relationship between humans and the figures they worship.

Getting hit by Cupid's arrow could render you totally besotted, or hating their guts. Best not get on his wrong side! This is *Cupid Tormenting the Soul* by John Gibson, 1837–1839, and he's at the Walker Art Gallery in Liverpool, UK.

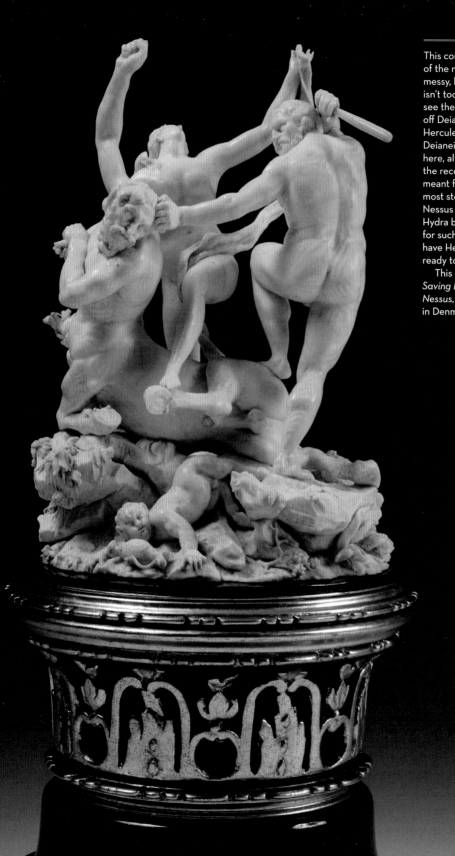

This could be a scene from the end of the night when the club gets really messy, like *really* messy. The reality isn't too far removed from that. We see the centaur Nessus trying to carry off Deianeira, Hercules's missus, and Hercules having none of it. It looks like Deianeira is putting up a good fight here, although she may have been on the receiving end of an errant blow meant for hubby Herc. According to most stories, Hercules overcomes Nessus with an arrow tipped with toxic Hydra blood, but that doesn't make for such a dynamic scene. Instead, we have Hercules with his trademark club ready to go into action.

This dynamic scene, titled *Herakles Saving Deianira from the Centaur Nessus*, comes from Rosenborg Castle in Denmark.

A contemporary critic in 1534 complained that this muscly Hercules looked like a sack filled with melons. Delicious!

Originally intended as a counterpoint to Michelangelo's *David*, this Hercules represents physical strength as a balance to the spiritual strength David displays and is another symbol of the city of Florence. However, things got a little bit complicated in the 1520–30s, with power changing in the city frequently. At one point, this statue changed from being Hercules to a biblical hero, Samson, but this was a brief blip, and this meloned muscled man became Hercules once more in 1530. He was completed in 1534.

This is not a happy story. And another example of Zeus being awful. So he visited Earth, and again saw a mortal he desired. This time he spied Leda, the queen of Sparta, as she bathed in a lake. Assuming the feathered form of a graceful swan, he swam up to Leda and, as he often did, refused to take no for an answer. The story goes that Leda laid a clutch of eggs, from which were born the heroes Castor and Pollux and the queens-to-be Helen (yes, that one) and Clytemnestra. According to ancient Greek travel writer Pausanias, the remains of Helen's egg became quite the tourist attraction.

Saints are important figures in the Christian Church. Saint Paul was one of the earliest people to spread the word of Jesus around the world. And, like many early saints, he was martyred for his faith. Paul was, as you can see, beheaded. In some accounts of his death, Paul's head bounced three times after being *separated* from his body, and each bounce brought forth a source of water. But that's by the by. It's clear that Taddeo Zuccaro wants us to see the executioner as a monster because that is one of the least flattering butts we've ever seen!

Mercury, or Hermes as he's also known, has had several careers since the whole "being-a-god-thing" didn't really pan out the way he thought. He's been a flower-delivery person, a high-end handbag designer, and the big boss behind a very dodgy parcel delivery company. It is good that throughout all these entrepreneurial enterprises he never skipped leg day.

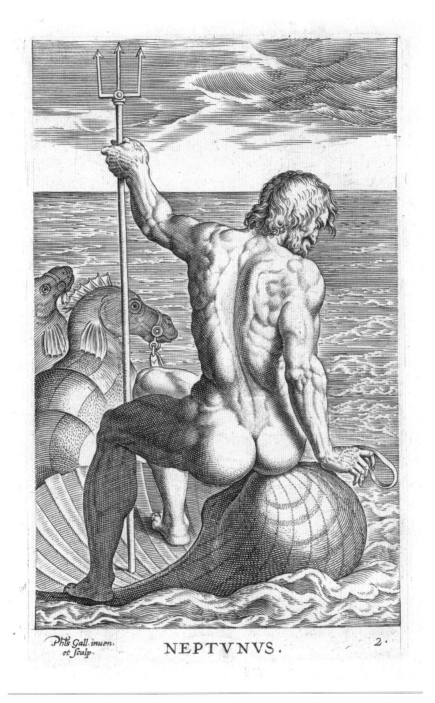

NEPTVNVS.

2.

That seashell does not look comfortable, but then we don't imagine couches survive very long underwater. Nevertheless, Neptune is making sure everything is fine before taking his seahorses out for a quick scallop.

Musicians really should know to empty their spit-valves.

Arms aloft, carefully aiming his formidable trident, is a common pose to see Poseidon striking. This silver coin is a tetradrachm, a Greek coin worth about four drachmae. These coins were first used in Athens, before being used throughout Greece. Poseidon was one of the gods who battled for patronship of Athens, but the people there decided that Athena's olive groves were more useful than a saltwater spring.

The story of Cupid and Psyche is the story of a soulmate romance, literally; Cupid is the personification of desire and Psyche's name means "soul." Cupid and Psyche's relationship gets off to a rocky start. People start worshipping Psyche instead of Venus, which draws the wrath of the goddess of love. Venus enjoys toying with Psyche and sets her several tasks, the last of which sends her into a deep, deathlike sleep. This statue shows Cupid reviving his soulmate, before he swoops her off to Olympus, where Zeus makes Psyche immortal and marries the happy couple, after warning Venus to leave her new daughter-in-law alone. Canova's statue is full of life and movement. Today, this energy makes the work eternally engaging, but when it debuted back in the late 1700s, a critic complained, "You must run around it, look at it from high and low, up and down, look at it again and keep getting lost."

Pygmalion did not care for any of the women in his town. So what's an artist to do? Why, create their own dream-girl, of course! Venus saw how much Pygmalion loved his newly created statue and turned the block of stone into warm, loving flesh. Jean-Leon Gerome's piece perfectly captures the moment of transformation, as cold unfeeling marble gives way to reveal the living girl. It takes a few centuries for the magical statue girl to be granted a name: Galatea.

Mermaids *can* have butts—it just depends on which half is the human half.

   Fishbutt Fandango by Sarah Hingley was exhibited at HOME Manchester, UK, in the first Manchester Open Exhibition in January 2020.

Please contact your nearest flamingo in the event that your amorphous blob unexpectedly gains sentience. It will find their presence soothing.

   The real monster lurking in Francis Bacon's work is the timeless agony of being human. Francis's works leave themselves open to interpretation, and *Figures in Movement* (1976) seems to explore ideas of fighting, being trapped, and being watched.

   France *is* Bacon.

According to some traditions, Hermaphroditus was the child of Hermes and Aphrodite and was one of the often mischievous minor love-gods known as the erotes, alongside Eros. According to others, Hermaphroditus is a merged being, a blend of the handsome youth Hermaphroditus and the nymph Salmakis, who refused to let him go. Whoever they are, what's in their pants is none of your business, and they're divine.

This is a photograph of a sleeping Hermaphroditus statue, a popular subject for sculptors. Sometimes the artist is so successful at crafting a comfortable-looking cushion that it causes audiences to give the cushion a cheeky prod to double-check that it is, in fact, made of stone. Hermpahroditus can be found in museums all over the world; this photo is from the Met, but Hermaphroditus can also be seen in the Vatican, Florence, and the Louvre in Paris.

Believe it or not, getting this tattoo was cheaper than buying a print of this from the museum gift shop. This is a "Psyche and Amour" tattoo on Captain Studdy, by Sutherland MacDonald, after William-Adolphe Bouguereau's *Cupid and Psyche*.

With their enthusiastic waving, soft and simple forms, and lack of monstrous features, Sir Edward Burne-Jones's sirens feel a million miles away from the mellifluous femmes fatales the seaside chanteuses are usually shown to be. EB-J's sirens also lack the other standard siren features; there are no wings and no fins and scales here, just human features.

Hylas was a beautiful young man who served as Hercules's arms-bearer and companion, and yes, that is a euphemism. He sailed with Hercules and a host of heroes on board the *Argo*, but he did not make it home. While resting, he was gazing into some water, and a group of sea-maidens, sometimes described as sirens, sometimes as naiads or water nymphs, saw how beautiful he was and dragged him under the waves to be with them forever. According to some stories, it was a happy-ever-after; according to others, his mouth was held shut to prevent him from crying out to Hercules. Either way, the episode has been a favourite one for artists for millenia. This example comes from the third century BCE, from a villa in Gaul, Roman France. It is on display in the Musée de Saint-Romain-en-Gal.

Do you think this artist has ever seen humans before? Come on, Adam, eat your fruit and veg!

Here's a prime example of religious art seeing bums as acceptable nudity; it's risqué but it's not obscene. And Eve and Adam are a unique example because their nudity is categorically unsexy—it's gospel!

Conclusive proof that mermaids have bums! Let your eyes follow the flow of the painting, from the mermaid's intense embrace of the young man, down her elaborately adorned hair, right down to the seafoam and her tail. Leighton certainly takes us on a journey of desire, of beauty, and to something much more sinister. The mermaid's embrace and kiss are mirrored by her tail entwining itself around and around the sailor's legs as she drags him to his doom. We are seeing this happen in slow motion; his bucket has already been upended, spilling its contents into the sea; it's only a matter of seconds before he joins her.

Theseus Fighting the Minotaur by Étienne-Jules Ramey (1796–1852) is a classic example of how the idealised approach to gods, monsters, and heroes can leave you feeling very, very conflicted. Neither battling bloke looks particularly bovine, and it's only by knowing that (spoiler alert) Theseus wins that we can work out which figure is which. The writhing wrestlers were made in 1826, and you can admire them from all angles in the Tuileries Gardens in Paris.

The robes flowing in the wind frame and swaddle Hermes's remaining features perfectly. How do we know it's Hermes? Because of his snazzy sandals, complete with wings—an essential feature for a messenger god. Hermes is resting his legs in the Greek town of Chalcis. Chalcis has an ancient history, with its earliest mention coming from Homer's epic poem *The Iliad*.

The legacy of classical sculpture, with their depictions of gods, heroes, and monsters, continues to influence artists today. This is Hal Fischer's *Archetypal Media Image: Classical*. It's not difficult to see the echoes of past sculptures in the pose the model takes. Fischer's work looks at archetypes, and stereotypes, and invites us to think about how we make meaning from images. It's worth pointing out that the text is as integral to understanding this piece as the image itself. Fischer's classical archetype here is part of his series called Gay Semiotics and was featured in the Met's "Camp" exhibition to complement the Met Gala theme in 2019. Fischer would like us to share that, for the record, he doesn't consider this image "camp."

ARCHETYPAL MEDIA IMAGE
CLASSICAL

THE CLASSICAL PROTOTYPE CAN BE VIEWED AS A MODERN CARICATURE OF ANTIQUE SCULPTURAL IDEALS. THE GAY MEDIA EMPLOYS THE CLASSICAL MOTIF RATHER EXTENSIVELY BECAUSE IT IS UNIVERSALLY UNDERSTOOD AND THEREFORE COMMERCIALLY VIABLE. THE SUBJECT IS USUALLY PRESENTED IN A HIGHLY DRAMATIC OR "SOCIALLY RECOGNIZED" ARTISTIC POSE, ROUGHLY COMPARABLE TO THE CLASSICAL AND DRAWING ITS LEGITIMACY FROM ITS ANTIQUE PREDECESSORS. THE SUBJECT IS USUALLY FULLY ILLUMINATED OR EDGE LIGHTING IS EMPLOYED WITH NO SCENERY OR PROPS AND A NEUTRAL BACKGROUND.

The first life-size nude marble statue of the Renaissance definitely deserves some attention, so let's take a look. Yep, there's the obligatory fig leaf and apple, so we know it's Adam. His face looks like he's supposed to be baking an apple strudel that serves twelve in thirty minutes and he's not entirely sure where to start.

You can definitely tell this statue was designed to be seen from the front. The back's smooth musculature and the odd "coiffed from the front but helmet-y from the back" hair tell us that perhaps the artist wasn't expecting us to be looking at Adam from behind.

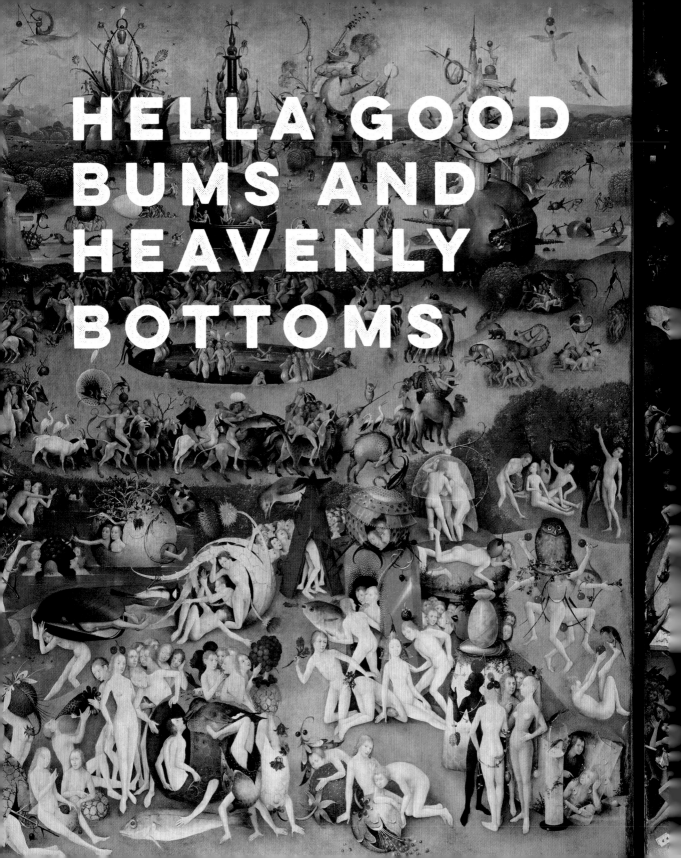

You know what hell has a lot of? Sinners. You know what organised religion wants you to think is sinful? Nudity. You know what nudity means? Butts! But if nudity is sinful, how come there are so many butts? Butts can be used to imply nudity and still get through the censors. After taking a bite of the forbidden fruit, Adam and Eve used fig trees to cover up their fronts but left their behinds free to enjoy a nice gentle breeze (see page 55).

But sinfulness is in the eye of the beholder. Nudity can represent innocence as well as naughtiness. The most beautiful of heavenly bodies can be as naked as any sinner; the only difference between them is whether they are being praised or punished.

And as even a casual art fan will know, it's not uncommon for art created for churches to end up in museums; churches, especially in Europe, have a lot of history, heritage, and stunning art. For a "going on a trip to see art" experience, you would do just as well visiting some churches as going to museums, and both can feed the soul in different ways. Churches are most definitely cultural spaces, so the art you'd see there would count as museum bums. We'd love to have expanded this chapter to look at bums in places of worship for other religions too, but quite honestly, that's a whole book's worth of religious bums!

Hieronymus, when we commissioned *The Garden of Earthly Delights*, we were expecting roses, an herb garden, and a nice parterre hedge maze . . .

Bosch's *The Garden of Earthly Delights* triptych is now part of the collection of the Museo Nacional del Prado, Madrid. This incredible piece has such a legacy reflected in other artists' work. Salvador Dalí's *The Great Masturbator*, 1929, bears an astonishing resemblance to one of the earthly delights; Joan Miró's *The Tilled Field*, 1923–1924, bears stark similarities. Surrealist painters René Magritte and Max Ernst took inspiration from Bosch, and some of the acts are even recreated on-screen in the 2004 film *The Garden of Earthly Delights*!

Heavenly Bottoms

When you look at art made for Christian spaces, bodies broadly fall into one of two categories: the hallowed or the harrowed. Representing the body glorious we have the work of Duncan Grant, an artist who was commissioned to decorate several churches in the UK in the twentieth century. His eye and his brush sought to show every muscle and sinew bathed in a heavenly light. Strength and power were tenets of "Muscular Christianity" (for more on the deification of the strong, able-bodied male form, flick to our chapter on "Beach Bums"). In 1953 Grant was commissioned to decorate the Russell Chantry in the ancient Lincoln Cathedral in the UK.

What do you think of his efforts?

Have a look at those sailors working on the docks. Unloading those heavy sacks should be strenuous work, and by rights they really should be sweaty messes. Hard work is a form of worship, after all. Grant's sailors, though, are glowing and glistening. All that physical labour is clearly doing a body good as well as a soul! Just look at that guy on the ladder. Swoon-worthy. It's a good thing this mural is behind the worshippers in the chantry because it would be hard to focus on praying with such a pert peach perched right there.

By this point in his career, Duncan Grant had built himself a reputation for making churches just a bit too sexy to function. Quite a skill, if you ask us.

The guy sitting down was supposed to be doing a stock check but was probably checking out all those thighs. Who can blame him?

Duncan Grant decorated the Russell Chantry in Lincoln Cathedral, UK, in 1953.

In 1941, Dunc and his fellow Bloomsbury Set member, Vanessa Bell, were commissioned to produce murals for St. Michael and All Angels, or as it is more commonly referred to, Berwick Church, in rural Sussex, England, only a stone's throw away from Charleston, their country retreat. According to letters written by Vanessa, it took Duncan a while to perfect his depiction of Christ. When discussing the project with a friend, Vanessa said: "We have got as far as doing sketches, which have met with approval on the whole, though D.'s Christ was thought a bit too attractive and my Virgin and bit frivolous." Duncan went through several versions before reaching a Christ that was just attractive enough without being a distraction to worshippers.

Duncan Grant clearly thought long and hard about heavenly bodies. God bless him for that.

Hellish Bums

Nice pictures of good people with glorious bodies are fine, but beauty can be bland after a while. Do you know what really hits home when sending a message? Terrifying grotesque pictures that will quite literally put the fear of God into your children if they don't do what they're told by the church.

Churches should be the last place where depictions of hell's dominion and all the bottoms therein should be, right? Short answer: no.

Longer answer: it's complicated. Churches have a history of controlling the narrative and presenting things in black-and-white terms. This was much easier for the church when their flock was largely illiterate and had a Lucifer's chance in heaven of understanding the Latin in any books they happened to see. You could tell them it meant whatever you wanted and they would have to just have faith that what you said was in their best interest. It also meant that the quickest way of telling stories and exerting that control was through pictures. Pictures on walls, pictures in windows, pictures hammered into the mountains of gold and silver that the church holds while still telling you they deserve charity. Ahem.

And by no means should anyone *enjoy* looking at these images. Art historian Georges Bataile said, "The Middle Ages gave eroticism its place in painting but relegated it to hell." He's talking about hellish torments and suggests the artists were relishing in their work. In all likelihood, it wasn't just the artists getting a bit of a thrill.

Let's take a look at Jan van Eyck's *The Crucifixion and The Last Judgement* (see page 64) on display at the Met in New York. The Met tells us that "every detail here is observed freshly and with equal interest." In the battle between good and evil, it is nice to see JVE is not playing favourites and his sinners are as much a focus as the heavenly hosts. Heaven is portrayed as good and orderly, with butts firmly on seats, whereas hell is chaos, with butts thrown in all sorts of directions with wild abandon. When thinking about this piece, art historian and chief curator at the Metropolitan Museum of Art Bryson Burroughs writes that "the diabolical inventions of Bosch and Brueghel are children's boggy lands compared to the horrors of the hell [van Eyck] has imagined." Don't worry, we'll get to Bosch.

What sets JVE's hell apart from the other artists is that his sinners aren't anonymous; his doomed and damned include kings and clergy. Nowadays we are more comfortable seeing the rich, famous, and powerful as sinners, the same as the rest of us, but in the 1400s, this was a radical statement to make.

Art historians aren't too sure whether this scene was meant for a public or private place of worship, but they seem to agree that it was for a place of worship nevertheless. At the moment it is on display where thousands of people can look at it every day, but it may have been intended for a much smaller audience. If it was meant for a private chapel, it's likely that the radical views in the painting would have been shared by the family who owned it. Thinking about the intended audience for an artwork can completely change how we interpret the little details.

As Gerald hung from the underside of the terrifying, giant, winged skeleton demon, he reflected, "Still not the worst party I've been to . . ."

This is a crop from Jan van Eyck's *The Crucifixion and The Last Judgement*, c. 1440, which is now on display at the Met, New York.

Devilishly Handsome

Would you like to hear a story about the Devil having too beautiful a bum for Liège Cathedral? Imagine you're Joseph Geefs, a sculptor in nineteenth-century Belgium. You're known for sculpting gorgeous young men. Liège Cathedral commissions you to sculpt Lucifer as part of the stone pulpit. You diligently carve and proudly present your finished Lucifer (right).

The officials blush and titter, they have confusing feelings in the pits of their bellies, and you can practically see the love-hearts in their eyes. Uh-oh. You made Lucifer too pretty! The Devil will definitely divert the attention of the congregation from the ponderous pontification of the long, dull sermons and, what's more, the clergy can't even see him from where they're standing on the pulpit.

Swoons We've never met a Lucifer more in demand. Created in 1842, Joseph Geefs's *Lucifer* was commissioned for the pulpit of Saint Paul's Cathedral, Liège, Belgium. Luci was removed from the cathedral before March 1844 for being too damned handsome. He was then acquired by King William II of the Netherlands (we don't know what for . . .). When the royal collection was dispersed in 1850, it was purchased by an art dealer from the Hague. Now he holds court in Belgium's Musées royaux des Beaux-Arts.

The cathedral requests a do-over. Perhaps Joseph's brother, Guillaume, could have a go instead.

Guillaume clearly has a strong sense of humour because his replacement Lucifer probably needs a "Parental Advisory: Explicit Content" sticker, he's smoking hot! he's flaming gorgeous! he's devilishly handsome!

After all that palaver, the clergy chose to welcome sexy Luci (Guillaume's version) into the cathedral, and Joseph's less-sexy-but-still-too-much-for-the-church version was exhibited publicly before ending up in the Royal Museums of Fine Art of Belgium.

Perhaps one of the most beloved infernal museum bums is Jacob Epstein's *Lucifer* at Birmingham Museum and Art Gallery (see page 80). The most beautiful of all the angels, this Lucifer was specifically designed to be androgynous and display different characteristics from different angles. We're getting late-1990s vibes from their low-rise waistband and we're here for it.

What's That Doing There?

When it comes to cheeky bums in churches, it's not just the Devil having all the fun. Non-Christian images and symbols have been snuck into church designs by artists and architects. Was it just for the thrill of getting away with it, or were the artisans and craftspeople who were doing the actual construction of the churches subverting the power of the chaps running the places? We'll never know because they are quite literally hidden histories. Heavily obscured histories at the very least. Probably the most well-known examples of these are busty mermaids and representations of the leafy-faced fertility god known as the Green Man carved on misericords (found under the wooden pews of the clergy). And let's not forget the many, many bottoms (see pages 68–70).

As churches get their once-in-a-two-hundred-year high-rise vacuuming, we're discovering more and more subversive images. Snuck into high-up wooden carvings and stained-glass windows that could never have been seen from the ground are bums aplenty. Glorious. It's easy to imagine Ethel and Arthur arguing over whose turn it is to host the raffle while a six-hundred-year-old man has got his goolies out and is spreading his cheeks 50 m above them (see page 70).

Fun fact: all the way back in 1998, vicar Father Andrew Mottram suggested selling postcards of this cheeky chappy to raise money for the church. It's a shame his idea was shut down; it would have made them a fortune by now!

What Is *That* Doing *There*?

You didn't think we'd write a chapter about representations of bums in hell without dedicating a sizable chunk to Hieronymous Bosch and his terrifying, hilarious, unsettling, unforgettable altarpiece *The Garden of Earthly Delights* did you?

Hieronymus Bosch was a fifteenth-century Dutch artist. That's pretty much all we know about him for certain. Oh, and he was well practiced at painting bums. *The Garden of Earthly Delights* is one of his most famous works (now in the Museo Nacional del Prado in Madrid). It provides us with an abundance of bums. It was created as an altar triptych, three paintings designed to be seen as one piece, putting all these butts in the holiest bit of a church. Looking closely at Rony B's work reveals what he thinks hell is: having flowers stuck up your bum, a threesome inside shellfish, music scribed onto your bottom by a devil with a very long tongue . . . no judgement! The more you look, the more you see. Rony must have had an imagination for sin.

Bosch's bottoms have caught popular attention for centuries. In 1990, Robert Gober created *Untitled* (see page 75) after being inspired by Rony's musical bum. More recently, a Tumblrer, known only as "Amelie," put the effort in and transcribed Bosch's backside ditty and presented the melody on their page. The thing we most love about this is that they stipulated it should be played on the kazoo, the king of musical instruments. Ideally, it would be played by a world-class tooter.

The bottoms in this chapter are all linked by ideas of heaven and hell; of saints, sinners, and all of us who sit somewhere in between those two extremes. When you flick through the bums, think about who would have seen them when they were new and who can see them now. Does it change what you think of them? Think about whether the bottoms represent innocence or whether the display of backsides represents the corrupting influence of hell.

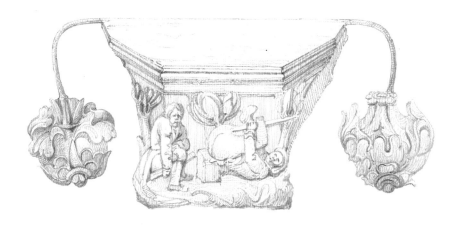

Who would have guessed that the bums were under the seats as well as on top them?

Proof perfect that you'll find more than just chewing gum under your chair if you're sitting in a church! Top: Location, Oude Kerk Amsterdam. Bottom: French School, fifteenth century.

"Wheeeeeeeeee."

This gentleman sliding down the hammerbeam roof features at All Saints Church, Hereford, UK, and is estimated to have been carved in the fifteenth century.

There are many, many, many bottoms on show in Bosch's *The Garden of Earthly Delights* (see the full image on page 60, think of the following pages as a highlights reel).

Butt Song
Adapted from Hieronymus Bosch's Garden of Earthly Delights

ChaosControlled123   Hieronymus Bosch

All together now, on three; one, two, three . . . *deep breath*

Robert Gober had a grand retrospective in 2007 at the Schaulager Museum in Basel, Switzerland, including this one, which is called *Untitled* and not *Everyone Loves a Musical Bottom*.

How to get to hell with murder from none other than Cain and Abel. Squabbling brothers Cain and Abel appear in Jewish, Christian, and Muslim sacred texts (and Neil Gaiman's *The Sandman Chronicles*) as two sons of Adam and Eve. Cain commits the first ever murder (of Abel) and is sent to hell (this is the very simplified version, btw, we're trying to keep it light!), and as is the wont of Renaissance painters, they're obvs naked while they're doing it (murdering/being murdered).

Johann Sadeler I's *Cain murdering Abel* from 1576 is at the Met Museum in New York.

This is Svend Rathsack's *Cain and Abel* from 1910. We haven't got anything different to say about this version of Cain and Abel, we just wanted to meet our bums quota for this chapter.

Completed in 1526, the *Last Judgement* now resides in the Stedelijk Museum De Lakenhal, Leiden, after being rescued from Pieterskerk during riots in 1566.

Fun how there are more bums among the heavens than there are in hell!

We just want to draw your attention to this prudish angel from the Van Leyden!

Putting Jacob Epstein's androgynous *Lucifer*, 1945, in their Round Room gives visitors to Birmingham Museum and Art Gallery the opportunity to see the most beautiful of all the angels from all angles, including (luckily for us) from behind!

The *Angel of the North* by Antony Gormley, 1998. At 20 m from head to foot (and 54 m from wingtip to wingtip), our Ang surely has the biggest angelic bum! Hallelujah!

It goes without saying, if you're going to slay a dragon, please wear some armour. At the very least, some oven mitts.

Edward Burne-Jones's *Study for St. George slaying the Dragon*, 1865–1866, Birmingham Museum and Art Gallery, UK.

This etching is all that remains of a painting by Paul Rubens that was destroyed by fire in 1740. We'll just have to imagine these devilish bottoms rendered in paint and colour.

It's Halloween and all the bedsheets are already taken!
Pierre Subleyras's *Charon Passing the Shades*, c. 1735, the Louvre, Paris.

For this one to make sense you've got to know that Orpheus was a master musician, and also had a brush with the underworld, being the only mortal to visit on a return journey.

Charles H. Niehaus's *Orpheus*, 1916 (though it was actually erected on June 14, 1922. June 14 is "Flag Day" in America, and Orpheus was to celebrate the centennial of the writing of the "The Star-Spangled Banner" in 1816).

Jennifer remembered her etiquette lessons and rode the goat sidesaddle on the way to the coven meeting.
Luis Ricardo Falero's *Witches Going to Their Sabbath*, 1878.

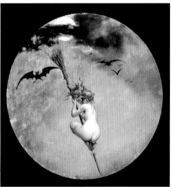

When it's 2 a.m. and the club's DJ is failing to get everyone to join in with "YMCA."
For an added meta-Museum Bum, this William Blake illustration was commissioned by Thomas Butts!
Satan Arousing the Rebel Angels by William Blake, 1808.

The Witch by Luis Ricardo Falero, 1882, painted on a tambourine because why not.

Picture this: you're walking around a museum and you see an image of two people, perhaps a man and a woman. They are sitting near each other, but their body language suggests they are, at best, indifferent to one another. The scene is entitled *The Lovers*. You move on. So what?

You come to another image of two people. This time they are the same gender. Perhaps they are two women. They are entwined with one another, or perhaps holding hands, or sharing a warm embrace. Perhaps the image is more abstract and you can only make out a mess of intertwining limbs. The image is called *The Friends* or maybe *The Companions*. The label goes on at length to explain how we could not possibly know the relationship between these two women. Who knows what kissing, cuddling, and holding hands could possibly signify?!

Museums are still hesitant to talk about same-sex attraction. Some are getting better and more confident with the topic, but in many cases the histories of LGBTQIA+ people from the past are only spoken of thanks to the efforts of particularly enthusiastic staff and volunteers who feel empowered to share it. Even then, these stories are usually only brought to the fore during LGBTQIA+ History Month or Pride season rather than being shared throughout the year.

"They're just good friends!!!" is the exclamation we've heard over and over again when we see overwhelmingly queer-flavored works of art in museums, but the curator/the institution/the manager who's just a little bit

Charles Demuth's *Dancing Sailors*, 1917, at the Cleveland Museum of Art. Even though the sailors are dancing with women, this is a painting with a queer love story in it. Follow their eyelines!

If you like this, look up Charles Demuth's other work; there are so many paintings of beautiful queer people, and his urban landscapes are . . . *chefs kiss* <3.

uncomfortable with the word *queer* doesn't want to celebrate, or even acknowledge that there might be something LGBTQIA+ going on. It's become a bit of a meme, with subjects of sapphic-centric works being described as "Gals Being Pals."

Imagine how art, culture, museums, and the world would be different if fragile straight men—and it is almost universally this group—hadn't had to make themselves more comfortable by erasing those who did not fit their narrow view of the world. If queer people and allies didn't have to work extra hard today to reverse those efforts so we could highlight and share and celebrate the queer stories in our collections. If we didn't have managers who wanted us to prove indefinitely that a queer historical figure definitely was definitely definitely queer because making that claim *still, in the roaring 2020s,* has shame and danger and taboo around it. Wouldn't that be nice?

Queer histories are an integral, valuable, and a legitimate part of actual history, not a niche topic to be set aside into specific gallery tours, to its own shelves of libraries, to its own distinct modules at college. These histories have been left out because, for a long time, there were laws against being LGBTQIA+, and even at the time of writing, anti-LGBTQIA+ legislation is still being introduced and debated in countries that consider themselves "civilised." Where LGBTQIA+ people from the past are clearly present and loud and proud and here and queer, they should be acknowledged and celebrated as such.

And besides, how are the straights ever going to learn any better if we don't gift wrap and bottle-feed our stories for them?

"But how do you know that there's something LGBTQIA+ going on?" The answer is often as simple as: just look! It can be as easy as that to see that the subjects are more than "just friends." However, curators try to argue that there isn't enough evidence to describe the subjects as LGBTQIA+ because it's not explicit (and when it is explicit, it's deemed damaging to morals—Won't somebody think of the children??—and so is hidden away. We just can't win!) Increasingly, this kind of rebuttal falls away when it's clear that it requires Olympic-level mental gymnastics to distort and deny the evidence in front of our eyes . . . and the artist's statement . . . and the account the subjects gave about their deeply passionate relationship with the other person.

Let's all enjoy some dancing sailors (see page 86). It's the early 1920s. The sailors are in port in New York City. The bars are hopping and a good time is being had by all. Charles Demuth is observing the goings-on in Greenwich Village, recording what he witnesses in watercolours, only for his paintings to be hidden away. In the image on pages 86–87 we see three couples dancing. Two of the couples show a male sailor dancing with a woman, and the central couple is male sailors dancing together. The women are not the focus of this piece; they are a pair of lips and a pair of eyes respectively, and their muted palettes blend them into the blurry background all too easily. No, our focus is on the sailors on the left and in the middle. Demuth clearly had his eye on their physicality and their well-tailored uniforms, but he also had an eye for capturing a story. Look at the way they are gazing at each

Gerda Wegener's *A Summer Day*, 1927, was part of an exhibition at Arken Museum of Modern Art, in Ishøj, Denmark, in 2015–2016, which coincided with the release of *The Danish Girl* in cinemas, about Lili Elbe's relationship with G. W. We think it's a shame accordions didn't play a bigger role in the film.

other. The sailor on the left has positioned his partner in such a way that he's able to gaze at the middle sailor. The middle sailor's dance partner clearly knows what's going on.

Around the same time as Demuth was watching the sailors in New York, Gerda Wegener was painting in Denmark. See above. Gerda's works are known for their progressiveness and the radical way they approach gender and sexuality. Gerda studied art at the Royal Danish Academy of Fine Arts, where she met her future spouse and muse, Lili Elbe. Lili was also a painter and featured in many of Gerda's

works. Lili's name may be familiar to you, as she was the subject of the film *The Danish Girl*. Gerda's paintings of Lili brought her success and acclaim in Paris.

Gerda shows the women she depicts as powerful and sensual, subverting the objectification of the traditional male gaze by empowering rather than objectifying her subjects. In *A Summer Day* (1927) we see some very obvious flirting going on between the comely accordion player and the woman carrying the flowers. The way Gerda has used the sunbeams to highlight this line of sight tells us that this is what we should be paying attention to.

Hopefully we're not the first people to point out that classical histories are full of same-sex attraction stories. Unfortunately, a succession of fragile straight men thought society at large just couldn't handle hearing about queer people (and gods, and creatures in between) living their lives, getting into dire straits, and loving with impunity, so they decided to "sanitise" (not our word) the translated texts to fit with their own worldviews. Cowards! They use euphemism at best and innuendo at worst to downplay the same-sex attraction present in the objects and artefacts that have come down to us from the classical world. "Favourites," "companions," and, of course, the old refrains of "They're just friends" and "We couldn't possibly fathom the true nature of the relationship" come back again and again.

Let's look at Achilles and Patroclus. The particularly fetching example on page 91, *Achilles Removing Patroclus's Body from the Battle,* is by Léon Davent, c. 1547. Achilles and his paramour have been popular figures in art ever since Homer started telling his stories about the Trojan War. Homer portrays the relationship between the two warriors as deep, tender, and meaningful, a stark contrast to the prickly persona Achilles adopts when dealing with pretty much every other character he encounters. While Homer doesn't explicitly say they are lovers, he does little to give any evidence to the contrary, and the theme of them being more than just friends is picked up by several other Greek writers like Aeschylus, Pindar, and Plato, who make it *very* clear. Aeschylus even has his Achilles praise Patroclus's thighs. (We agree with Aeschylus's Achilles.)

Unfortunately, the couple face a tragic end in mythology, with Patroclus dying in battle while dressed in Achilles's armour, and Achilles running amok and slaughtering Trojans left, right, and middle before Paris hits him in his pesky heel with that arrow. However, their ashes are interred together, meaning that they are embracing for all eternity. Totally normal for "just friends . . ."

Achilles and Patroclus are part of a pattern of warrior heroes being more than just friends. You've heard of David and his gigantic battle with Goliath, but have you read the bit of the Bible where David and his boyfriend Jonathan have souls that are bonded together, have love for each other "over the love of women." David, like Achilles, is another favourite subject of artists; in fact, thanks to Michelangelo, he might be one of the most famous Museum Bums ever. You can see David's divine derriere on pages 42–43.

Fortunately, things are generally getting better. More and more LGBTQIA+ histories are being found in the collections, archives, and historical records and these stories are being increasingly shared, highlighted, and celebrated by museums, galleries, and cultural spaces. As you flick through the following bums, bottoms, and butts, consider whether you think the subjects are "just friends," and then keep that in mind the next time you're in a museum.

Achilles Removing Patroclus's Body from the Battle (and for some reason, Patroclus's clothes . . . Not the right time for a cuddle, Achilles!) by Léon Davent, c. 1547, from the collections of the Met in New York.

Yup, stage three of grief is the never-recommended DIY haircut.

Henry Fuseli's *Achilles Sacrificing His Hair on the Funeral Pyre of Patroclus*, 1795–1800. Held by the Kunsthaus, Zürich.

Apollo and his human boyfriend, Hyacinthus, were playing catch, and Apollo's godly throw accidentally bonked Hy on the head and instantly killed him. Even the mighty god of healing couldn't bring his bae back, so where his blood spilled, the flowers that grew were thence known as hyacinths. Here's Apollo taking Hy along for a fly, with lyre and shield in tow.

Despite the gazillions of examples in art and literature showing Apollo and Hy's intense love affair, some very confused historians have tried to claim they are merely "friends."

This image is by P. Aquila, after Annibale Carrace, c. 1670, from the Wellcome Collection in London, UK.

Ampelos was the personification of the grapevine, so Bacchus (god of wine) was naturally very fond of him. Ampelos was a beautiful satyr youth, who died from being on the pointy end of a bull. Overcome with grief for his beloved, Bacchus (Dionysus if you're Greek) transformed Ampelos into the first grape and vine, and made wine from him . . . Awwww . . . ?

By the way, there's another Bacchus we want to talk about. Sergius & Bacchus were Christian soldier saints who have recently been reinterpreted as queer lovers. These were the epitome of "close friends," where there's overwhelming evidence that they're in a relationship but the powers that be can't handle that, so they'd prefer you to think they're just good friends. (But we can't find any pictures of them from museums that are particularly bum-y.)

Anyway, Bacchus and Ampelos are here at the Rijksmuseum in Amsterdam.

Harmodius and Aristogeiton are so solidly known as gay lovers and a couple that even the fustiest of curators finds it difficult to ignore. The Athenian lovers assassinated Hipparchus, the "last tyrant of Athens," in c. 527 BCE by hiding daggers in his ceremonial wreath for the Panathenaic Games, but failed to assassinate his brother, who became the next tyrant of Athens . . . good try, boys!

Here they are at the National Archaeological Museum in Naples, Italy. The first version of this statue was made by Antenor before 480 BCE. That was stolen from Athens and moved to Susa. Alexander the Great returned it to Athens, in 477 BCE, but it has now disappeared. Kritios and Nessiotes were commissioned to make a replacement, and the lovers stood side by side in the Agora until at least 200 CE. Those are also lost now, but many copies were made from them, the best of which is in the photo! Basically, these are popular guys (unless you're a tyrant).

When your friendship group can't decide between bottomless brunch and a burlesque night. Art historians aren't entirely sure what's going on here. It's probably just a study rather than an actual battle. However, it's the earliest depiction of a male nude in the Renaissance. There's lots of fun symbolism in the picture, like the central fighting pair sharing a linked chain, possibly revealing that these two are having a lovers' tiff.

Battle of the Nudes by Antonio del Pollaiuolo, c. 1470, resides at the Cleveland Museum of Art, USA.

Herc and Iolaus here, beating their snakes.

Some people say that Iolaus was Herc's nephew. Plutarch says that Iolaus was Herc's lover, and the nephew story was to explain their closeness. There is a shrine to Iolaus in Thebes, which was sacred to same-sex couples, and where they prayed together and made vows to each other.

As you can probably tell, Iolaus gave Herc a hand with defeating the Hydra. Iolaus did the cauterising while Herc did the chopping off of heads, meaning they eventually overcame the beast and Herc accomplished his second labour.

This is by Hans Sebald Beham, 1545, and it's at the Rijksmuseum, Amsterdam.

Hyacinthus, the guy who Apollo accidentally killed with a wayward discus, was also admired by Zephyrus, a god of the wind. The alternative version of the story is that Zephyrus is actually responsible for Hy's death because he directed the wind to serve Apollo's discus towards Hy. He was jealous that Hy had chosen Apollo over himself (and Boreas, the god of the north wind, and Thamyris, a mortal man . . . !) So it was very much an "If I can't have you, no one can" situation!

As you can see, they were *very* close. These cuddly boys are from c. 490 BCE, from ancient Greece, at the Museum of Fine Arts in Boston, USA.

Look at these two gorgeous figures . . . *swoon*

Nisus and Euryalus are inseparable lovers, fighting together in Virgil's *Aeneid*. Euryalus's shiny helmet (!) attracts the attention of the enemy, which leads to the death of both, which is what Jean-Baptiste-Louis Roman is depicting in this statue. Moral of this story is if you're doing a sneak attack, use camouflage!

Special thanks and credit to the Louvre, which pulled out all the stops to get a nice photo of these butts <3.

Your cats watching you dance naked around your house, making a note to bring this up at your next appraisal. The famous Orpheus story is his botched attempt to retrieve Eurydice from the underworld. What is less well known is that after Eurydice is definitely and finally dead, Orpheus lives his best bisexual life. The women of Thrace literally pulled Orph apart because he wouldn't pay them attention, he was more into the boys.

John Macallen Swan's *Orpheus*, 1896, at the Lady Lever Art Gallery in Liverpool, UK.

There was one particular Thracian gent that Orpheus was "very good friends" with. Calais was on Orph's mind while he had a little walk through the countryside. While thinking beautiful thoughts about Calais like a post-Brexit Brit, Orph didn't notice the angry ladies who ambushed and killed him.

This is *Orpheus* by Cristofano da Bracciano, 1600, at the Metropolitan Museum of Art in New York.

We have to commend these chaps on their being completely relaxed about the possibility of splinters!

This is *Untitled* by Alvin Baltrop, who photographed queer men at the Hudson River piers in the 1970s and 1980s. During his life, his career suffered from racism and homophobia, and he only achieved international fame after his death in 2004. You can find his works in the collections of the Whitney Museum of American Art and the Met.

Jeff, you really need to get rid of those socks, they're full of holes!

Paul Cadmus's "magic realism" was a mixture of gritty social commentary and eroticism. One of his paintings was described as "unnecessarily dirty," but not this one, because there's soap.

Paul Cadmus's *The Bath*, 1951, from the Whitney Museum of American Art, New York.

"Cycling wedgies are the worst."

Abraham Janssens had a wife and eight children, but also demonstrated his strong appreciation for the male form in his paintings. We won't be accepting any potential bi-erasure here, thank you very much!

This is *The Penitent and Impenitent Thieves*, 1611, from the Museum de Fundatie, Zwolle, in the Netherlands.

Much replicated and reproduced, this statue has been very popular with a certain corner of queer culture ever since the original appeared in ancient Greece, and could explain where baby wrestlers come from? These wrestlers can be found in the Accademia Ligustica di Belle Arti and are based on a Roman copy of a lost Greek original.

OUDE STEEN TE BORDEAUX GEVONDEN.

Another problematic queer couple from classical antiquity. What a shock. Here we see Zeus as an eagle with his "cupbearer," Ganymede. "Cupbearer" wasn't a position Ganymede applied for, but one that was thrust upon him. This episode is often known as "the rape of Ganymede." This is but one of Zeus's crimes.

Antieke Steen, 1776–1851, Daniël Veelwaard (printmaker), after Pierre Lacour (artist). Rijksmuseum, Amsterdam.

Always aggravating when you want to join in but can't get the stupid shirt off in time.
Wrestling Match, 1649, Michiel Sweerts, Staatliche Kunsthalle Karlsruhe, Germany.

A bonus bum in the frame decoration, and again, Zeus (in the guise of an eagle), taking the shepherd boy Ganymede without consent up to Olympus to serve at his pleasure . . .
Ganymede and the Eagle, 1921, John Singer Sargent, Museum of Fine Arts, Boston, USA.

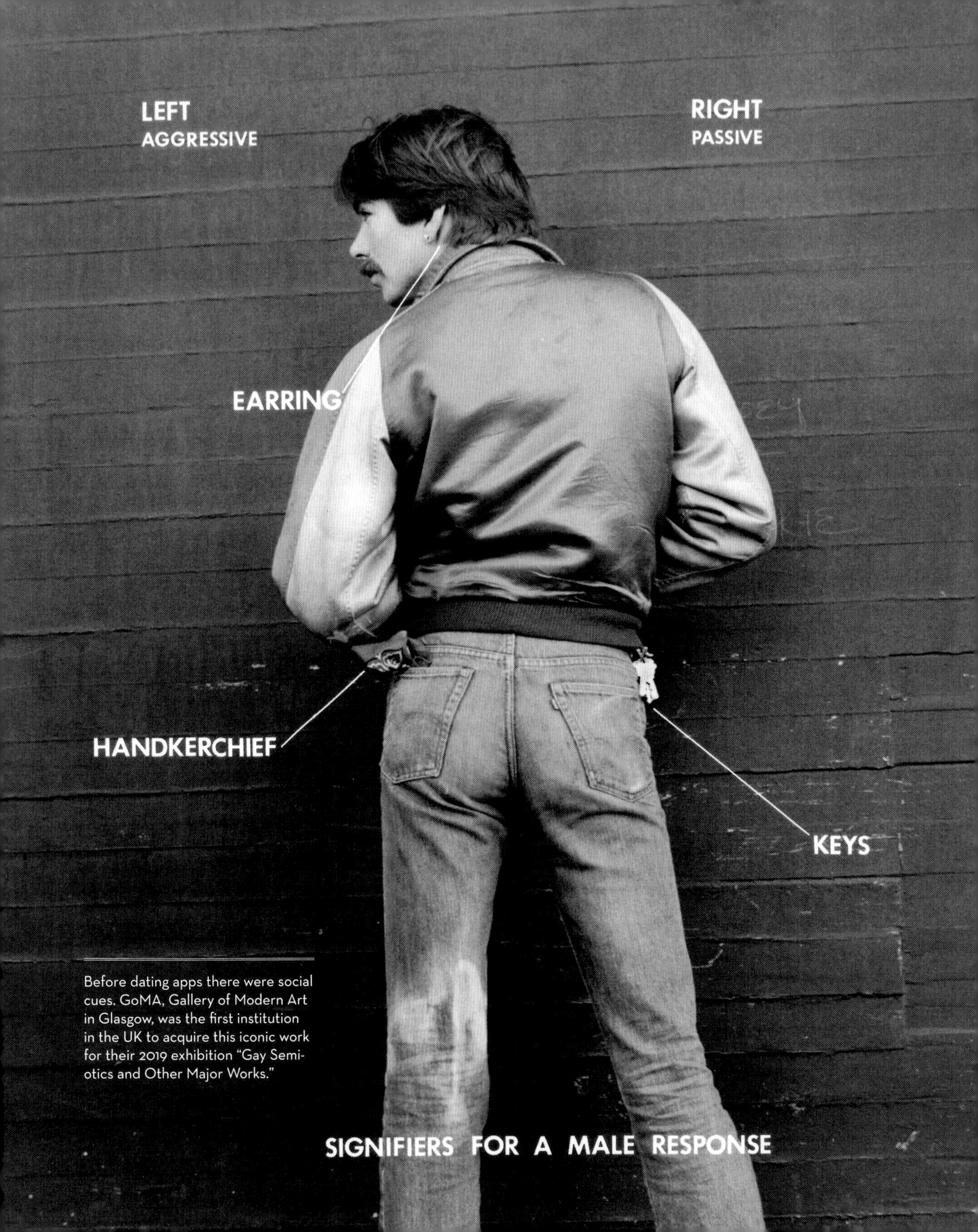

LEFT
AGGRESSIVE

RIGHT
PASSIVE

EARRING

HANDKERCHIEF

KEYS

Before dating apps there were social cues. GoMA, Gallery of Modern Art in Glasgow, was the first institution in the UK to acquire this iconic work for their 2019 exhibition "Gay Semiotics and Other Major Works."

SIGNIFIERS FOR A MALE RESPONSE

Peaches are not the only fruit; here are some apricots also bursting with bumminess.

WHEN IS A BUM

NOT A BUM?

Bums, butts, and bottoms might seem like a fun and frivolous topic, but if you've made it this far into the book, you can see that in our study of bums we aren't afraid to ask the big questions about the universe. Is beauty truth? Is truth beauty? And perhaps the most important question of all: When is a bum not a bum? When is a bum simply in the eye of the beholder? Humans are predisposed to see faces in things that definitely aren't faces. Spotting Jesus in your toast or seeing a very good Labrador in your floorboards are classic examples of this. It's called *pareidolia*, and it's how our brains are wired to help us make sense of the random stimuli we are bombarded with constantly. After years of looking for bums, we can find them in museums everywhere, even where no one's ever expected or intended a bum to be.

That vase? That's a bum. This piece of modern art? Eighteen bums. You thought you were looking at a candlestick? Oh my dear, no, that's very definitely three butts in a trench coat masquerading as a candlestick.

You might be thinking that we, the authors of *Museum Bums*, a book about butts in museums, might have a vested interest in telling you that things that aren't necessarily bums in museums are actually bums in museums. But as you're about to see, no matter what museum or cultural space you visit, you *will* get distracted by bums. Here we've got negative space bums, things that evoke buminess while not being bums at all, and allegorical bums—where actual bums are just a bit too exciting for the audience, these are considered appropriate stand-ins.

Let's start with the things that aren't bums because they're shaped around the spaces where bums are supposed to be: negative space bums. You've definitely seen examples of chairs and benches that are carved, molded, hammered, and printed to form a mold of a bottom for maximum comfort.

Tokujin Yoshida's *Honey-Pop* (see page 104) is one such chair, so called because its paper structure looks not unlike a honeycomb with the way the pages are folded back and forth to give the chair its strength and structure. Yoshida is an artist whose work explores finding new uses for existing materials, in this case, turning paper used to make traditional lanterns into an innovative chair. Each chair Yoshida constructs is made up of 120 sheets of glassine paper. When the chair that was donated to the Victoria and Albert Museum was partially opened, Yoshida sat on it. The seat and the back conformed to his shape. He literally left an impression of his butt on his work! Oh to have been there at the creation and conception of such a Museum Bum! Yoshida's paper chairs mold to the body of the first person to sit in them, giving each owner their own custom chair built to their exact specifications. One sold at auction in 2020 with an estimate of $2,000.

Not a bum, but very definitely not *not* a bum.

The buminess of things can be seen in glassware, sculpture, fine art, everywhere. It doesn't even have to be in the collections. If your local museum has a particularly callipygian wainscotting . . . that's a museum bum! One of the first bums we ever posted on our socials was an unusual tumbler from Czech glassmaker and designer Pavel

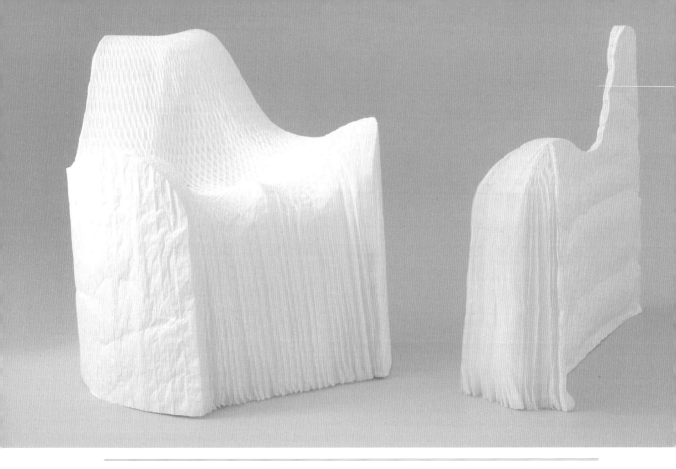

Would you like a seat that you can mould to your own bum by sitting in it? Tokujin Yoshioka opened and sat in his chair made from paper, after it was bought by the V&A, creating a unique seat to the exact specification of his own bum. Majestic!

Honey-Pop Armchair, 2000, Tokujin Yoshioka, Museum of Modern Art.

Hlava on display at London's Victoria and Albert Museum. That's definitely a bum.

It might come as a surprise, but our bottom-based pareidolia is not just confined to inanimate objects and places where an actual, real-life fleshy bum once was. It also affects how we look at some artworks that show people. Take a look at the painting by Edward Burra called *Soldiers at Rye* (see page 118). Is that a muscular arm or a global glute? Is that a bulbous back or a bootylicious backside? His figures can be a tangle of body parts, and the viewer has their work cut out to make

sense of what they're seeing. "Is it a bum or not a bum?" is a question to ask yourself with every glimpse, glance, and gaze at this piece. Burra has specifically given us a view of the soldiers from the back, perhaps to specifically encourage this question. Burra's painting is full of furtive energy and makes our eyes dart all over the scene, lingering on the parts that hold our interest the most: the backs, biceps, and bottoms of the military men.

Now, for the potentiality of a museum bum: there are also the not-bum-shaped pieces of art. They don't remind you of bums, but there's just something bum-relevant to them. When we see costumes and clothing in museums, it's only natural to imagine how they would have been worn and to think about what they might have looked like on the bodies they were designed for. Sporting heritage is not often highlighted in museums, and when we think generally about history and culture, sport is often seen as something separate. Take Tom Daley's Olympic diving trunks. Tom is a British gold-medal-winning Olympic diver, and he donated his signature swimwear to the Museum of London in 2013 to commemorate the London Olympic Games in 2012, in which he won a bronze as well as the heart of the UK (see page 115). The Olympic kit, designed by British fashion icon Stella McCartney, features a deconstructed and reimagined Union Flag. In their current form, these tiny trunks are not bum-shaped, but tell us you're not thinking of that Olympic-gold-medal-winning bottom right now!

Fun fact: Tom's trunks are especially tiny, not just because of his slim 28 in waist, but to avoid any unfortunate wardrobe malfunctions as he hits the water when he dives.

And then we have our allegorical bums. These are things that are definitely not bums but make you think of bums (and maybe they actually are bums): like those many, many, *many* paintings of peaches. One of the earliest representations of the peach in Western art comes from a fresco from Herculaneum, a town that was destroyed with Pompeii when Vesuvius erupted in 79 CE. It was a new, exotic fruit at the time, having its moment in the sun as the "it" thing to eat. It was the avocado on toast of the first century CE. Peaches have pretty much been a staple of diets and still lifes since then.

Ultimately we'll never know whether artists were thinking of pert, firm bottoms or they were just hungry, but the important thing here is that there is a possibility that bums were on their minds.

With its famous juiciness and distinctive shape, the peach has always been a symbol for something sensual going on. This

This is the oldest depiction of peaches in Western art. Despite their age, they have stayed pert and wrinkle-free. *Frescos of three vignettes of fruit*, Casa dei Cervi, Herculaneum, 45-79 CE. National Archaeological Museum of Naples.

has become clear since 2010 and the first appearance of our beloved iconic peach emoji. In fact, in 2016, when Apple redesigned their emoji line, they tried to make the peach look more like fruit and less like buttocks.

Whereas the peach's flesh gives it that *je ne sais quoi* that we enjoy so much here at *Museum Bums* HQ, it's the seed of the Coco-de-Mer plant that is a gift for us (see page 118). The Coco-de-Mer is a rare species of palm tree found in the Seychelle archipelago, and fun fact: as well as looking like a bottom, it is the largest known seed in the plant kingdom. Don't think it's just us whose brains see bums, though; Coco-de-Mer's scientific name is *Lodoicea callipyge*, which means "sea coconut of the beautiful buttocks."

Moore Than a Bum

The power of the bum is so great that it can transcend human form. Let's think about Henry Moore's *Large Two Forms* (see page 107). Henry Moore was a twentieth-century British artist most famous for his monumental bronze sculptures. Moore was creating work in a post–World War II landscape, when creators kept their eyes on the future because in looking back all they saw was war, destruction, and death. Moore was no exception. His huge bronze sculptures dot rural and urban landscapes around the world, and without fail they evoke *body*.

Across Moore's broad oeuvre, his work ranges from definitely traditional human shape to "I'm pretty sure that's an elbow, but what's it doing coming out of their big toe?" Henry Moore was a regular visitor to the British Museum, and he said he was influenced not by Greece and Rome, but by Mayan, Indian, and Mesopotamian styles, forms, and peoples. The influence his public art had on society helped usher in a new period of modernism in art and philosophy. You'd think this radical approach might ruffle some feathers in the art world, but Henry Moore was well respected, and what's more, he was well liked. Kenneth Clark, the author, broadcaster, and art historian, said: "If humankind were to send a single person to another planet to demonstrate the very finest qualities of our species, there would be no better ambassador than Henry Moore."

When creating *Large Two Forms*, Henry Moore thought deeply about how we see and think about the human form. They're definitely bodies in reclined forms, or huddles, or a couple in embrace. But they're also definitely not. We can't help but see hips, buttocks, crevices, crooks, dimples, and all the other constituent parts of bums. Some people also see the undulating forms of Moore's birthplace, the Yorkshire landscape (post-Jurassic volcanoes smoothed out by thousands of years of glaciers, referred to by locals as "God's Own Country"). Indeed, it's said that Moore was most happy seeing his sculptures in fields surrounded by sheep. Luckily, that's entirely possible today, as

Large Two Forms is at Yorkshire Sculpture Park, where there is a very good chance of seeing lambs gamboling around the art.

Sheep aside, there's something inherently sexy in Moore's big, bountiful curves and swerves. There's tension and physicality in his distinct forms, positioned so that they almost meet but are stuck for eternity, unable to bump beautifuls. You can see reflections of human sensuality in his sculptures specifically designed to look spiky and angular from one side and soft, smooth, and flowing from another. From this angle, that's certainly a bottom. Walk a few paces and suddenly your perspective sees something else entirely. Or does it?

As you peruse the following objects and artefacts that may or may not be bums, think about what the artist was trying to do. Is the bumminess an accident or something that was 100 percent intended?

Moore Moore Moore! How do you like it? How do you like it?

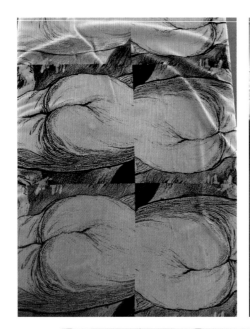

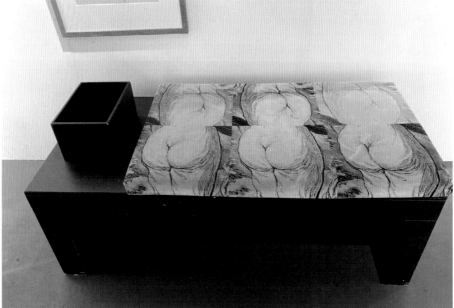

One of the best examples of bums that aren't bums but kind of are bums is this bench at the Cartoon Museum in London. While not bum-shaped in the slightest, the colourful cushion cover shows that this is, in fact, one of the bummiest objects in any museum because it has no fewer than six bums!

Before they became a cushion, these cheeks could be seen in a satirical print by cartoonist James Gillray called *The Graces in a High Wind*, a scene taken from nature in Kensington Gardens, made in 1810.

Hans Coper was one of the most celebrated ceramicists in the UK in the twentieth century. This piece, created in 1968, is a perfect example of the movement that revolutionised studio pottery through Coper's inventive use of form. We'd like four, please.

Clearly a bum. No further questions.
This is the *Bull's-Head Amulet* from the Cleveland Museum of Art, but originally from Egypt 5,500 years ago.

"Mooning," to bare one's bum, comes from sixteenth-century British slang, but the practice of mooning really came into prominence in the 1960s in American college frat houses.

Luke Jerram created *Museum of the Moon*, a giant 1:500,000 scale model of the moon, in 2016. The piece was floating in Bristol's harbour on a warm summer's evening in 2017. Proud Bristolians would share their love of this artwork by calling it "Proper Gert Lush," which means "Very Good Indeed."

From a pre-79 CE fresco from Herculaneum to modern-
day emojis, peaches have always brought bums to mind.
   The Museum of Modern Art in New York held an
exhibition in 2010 called "MoMA <3 Emoji."

Here's Kolman Helmschmid's *Portions of a Costume Armor* from c. 1525. As you can imagine from someone whose name was Helmschmid, he was pretty good, so this combined breastplate and backplate, with sleeves, was created to show off Kolman's skills in the smithy, not actually for fighting.

A similar piece was recently highlighted as part of the "Iron Men: Fashion in Steel" exhibition at Vienna's Kunsthistorisches Museum in 2022.

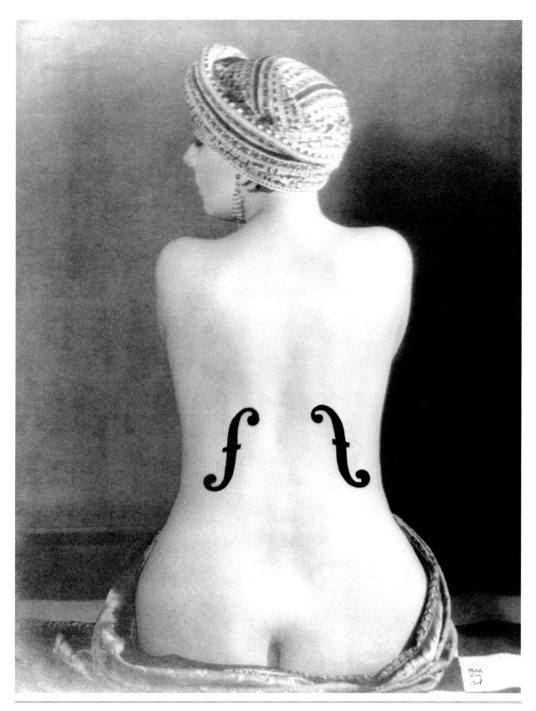

First published in 1924 in the surrealist magazine *Littérature*, Man Ray's famous *Le Violon d'Ingres* (*Ingres's Violin*) depicts his muse and lover, Kiki de Montparnasse, with violin holes painted on her back. An original print sold for a record-breaking $12.4 million in 2022. Now that's an expensive violin!

JD Fergusson was a young British creative who got swallowed up by Paris's passionate revolutionary community and returned to Britain with an entirely different outlook on art, beauty, freedom, truth, and love. A twenty-first-century catalogue entry for this painting timidly states that it "might at first seem to be an abstract image, but it probably represents a couple having sexual intercourse."

"Team GB" actually stands for "Team Great Butts."

These trunks represent an important part of British sporting heritage and were worn by Tom Daley in the London 2012 Olympic Games. They have been on display at the Museum of London since 2013.

Here's a bum that's not a bum. This 2,400-year-old wooden object was originally a delicate lathe-turned bowl, but now looks like a bum. It survived in waterlogged anaerobic conditions but got squashed into its peachy present-day appearance. While the vessel can't be shaped back into its original form, archaeologists have created a model that shows it pre-posterior. Iron Age pottery is rare in southwest Scotland, so perhaps these wooden bowls were common.

The *Black Loch Bowl* was discovered during excavations in 2018 at the Black Loch of Myrton, by AOC Archaeology Group, supported by Historic Environment Scotland and volunteers.

A reconstruction, showing the bowl unsmooshed.

Unrealistic beauty standards from the world of vases!

The imaginatively named *Vase*, 1913, by the imaginatively named "Taxile Doat," this round thing in your face is in the Saint Louis Art Museum.

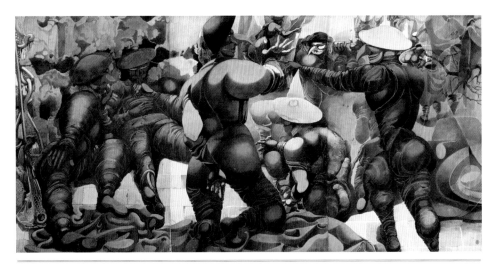

Edward Burra made sketches of soldiers when his hometown of Rye (usually quite sleepy) became a military centre in World War II. The distorted figures reflect Burra's engagement with the surrealist movement, which might explain why Burra's butts, biceps, and bulges all look the same.

Scientists literally named this seed "sea coconut of the beautiful buttocks." Really!

The Royal Academy of Arts in London held a special private opening for a naturist group to enjoy their "The Renaissance Nude" exhibition. So. Many. Bums.

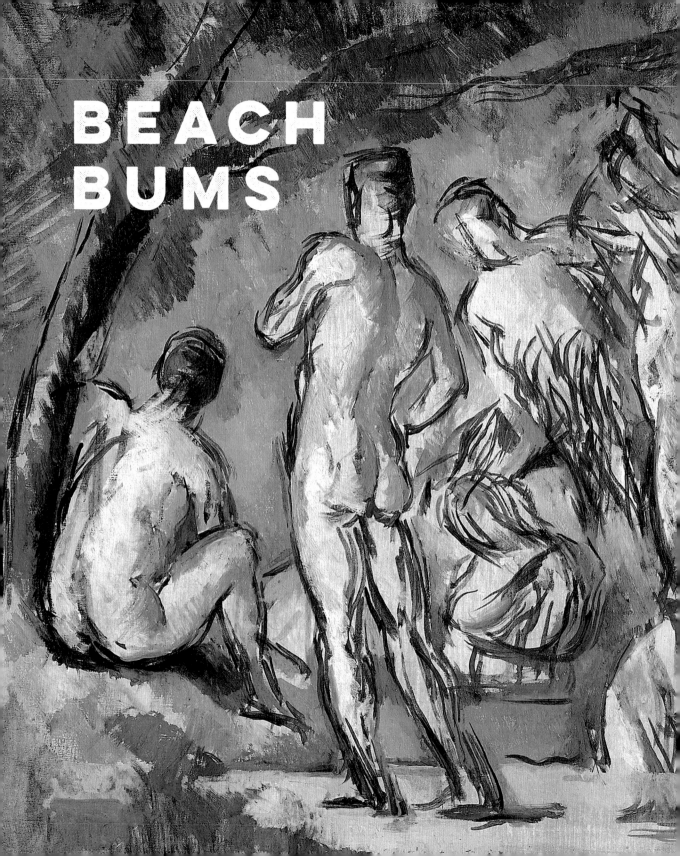

BEACH
BUMS

Just because museums are an indoor activity doesn't mean that we can't look at butts from the outside every now and then. Some of these wild, open-air bottoms even make it into our museums. A lot of wild, open-air bottoms share two very prominent features: they are attached to white boys and they're on beaches. It's easy to see the appeal of the beach: the warm sun beating down on you, the waves gently caressing the shore, that sea air making you feel alive. Even the sand that gets everywhere, and we mean everywhere, isn't enough to dampen how we feel about beaches. Also, the male form can be pleasant to look at from time to time.

But how did these sandy scenes make it into our museums?

The nineteenth century saw an explosion in the fashion for paintings of beaches and beachgoers. There are figuratively billions of them. We could write another book called *Beach Bums* that would contain hundreds of nineteenth-century paintings or sketches of a bebottomed person at the beach.

Why, though? What made this genre of painting so popular? The people who were rich enough to buy and commission paintings (or people who aspired to look like they were rich enough) generally lived in dirty, cramped industrial cities where everything was covered in a layer of soot. Seeing an image full of light and space and colours other than grey would do wonders for their mood.

These cities would have been full of unhealthy people cluttering up the place, all choking coughs and ghostly pallours.

Seven Bathers by Paul Cézanne, 1900, from the Beyeler Foundation.

Anyone who bared flesh was deemed to be doing so for immoral purposes, and those who lay down during daylight hours were probably addicted to opium. In contrast, these paintings offered a glimpse of clean, fresh, spacious, healthy, and relaxed living in a carefree seaside world, where the word *frolic* wrote itself in the surf with every cute little wave. In these quaint seaside idylls, nudity wasn't depraved, it was pure; sunbathing wasn't lazy, it was basking in the gods' natural wonders. Nudity, and the bare bottoms that came with it, were wholesome and natural, not seedy and unseemly.

Art appreciators' enjoyment of the bathing beauty isn't something that's just confined to the past, either. Famed British painter David Hockney depicted handsome young men lounging by swimming pools in LA in many of his major works from the 1960s and '70s, with *Peter Getting Out of Nick's Pool* (1966) being a favourite piece at *Museum Bums* HQ. Hockney's poolside works enabled him to bring up to date what he calls the "three-hundred-year tradition of the bather as a subject in painting."

Artists like Henry Scott Tuke and Paul Cézanne pitched up at the seaside and set about capturing this paradise in the newly fashionable *en plein air* style (this just means "outside"). They hired/borrowed/befriended young local men and convinced them to strip off and splash about in the shallows, or laze around miraculously retaining their pearly white complexion after hours modelling in midsummer sunshine. These men were workers. They didn't have the bodies they had because

they had gym memberships; they grafted in tin mines in Cornwall and worked farmland in Provence, France. They were the embodiment of the benefits of hard work.

Tuke was known as "par excellence the painter of youth," and you may notice just how youthful some of his models were. Several of them have been interviewed by students and academics who were interested in Tuke's work, and unanimously they said how they felt safe and secure, and everything was aboveboard. During the time Tuke was painting these young men, things that were generally considered normal and innocent, like nude sea-bathing, may now be thought of as suggestive. Tuke's art really makes these societal changes obvious and shows how things have shifted dramatically over time.

It could be quite possible that there is an underlying charged gaze in Tuke's work. It's easy for audiences today to interpret these images as erotic, and it's human nature to want to read into things and construct a narrative that fits what we want to see. To find out whether this is true or not, one option is to go right to the source. Unfortunately, Tuke's family destroyed much of his correspondence after his death. This may seem to be a strange thing for a family to do; surely scholars, critics, and fans would be very keen to know Henry's thoughts on things. However, this destroying of records is not as uncommon as one might think, and it was often done when relatives discovered that the deceased was LGBTQIA+.

Clever people are spending a lot of time arguing over whether these youthful, nude, muscled men are *supposed* to be sexy. You might think that the answer to this debate is obvious; today we have Calvin Klein ads and hunky superheroes telling us that yes, this imagery is supposed to be sexy.

The part that makes this more complicated is that in the nineteenth century, youthful, nude, muscled men could, really honestly, represent something else, like innocence, strength, simple working-class beauty, or how pretty the gods' creations are. But in truth, the answer is probably a bit of both.

Around this time, there was a metaphorical and literal deification of youth, whiteness, and physical fitness. In some of Tuke's works, we see young men striking poses that come straight from ancient Greece and Rome. They are taking on the roles of gods and heroes: mimicking Meleager, posing like Perseus, and masquerading as Hercules. The eighteenth and nineteenth centuries saw a resurgence in the fashion for classical architecture, philosophy, and standards of beauty. This is why your local civic museum building has fluted columns and looks like it came from ancient Greece. Exciting Victorian excavations at Pompeii helped kickstart a craze for returning to what was considered the height of civilised culture from the ancient Romans and Greeks, and this included seeing classical art as the best art, to be revered, collected, copied, and inspired by.

But Tuke wasn't just inspired by Greeks and Romans. In 1923, he travelled to the West Indies with some friends, one of whom was an inspiration for everyone's favourite archaeologist, Indiana Jones.

While Tuke was in the West Indies, he continued to sketch and paint the strapping young lads he saw by the seashore. Tuke's work from this time was displayed in the Royal Academy but didn't enthrall the London audience like his other work. Tuke's sister wrote that "people clearly preferred his Cornish models." Without Tuke's own thoughts on the differences between his paintings of white boys from Cornwall and Black boys in the West Indies, we'll never know their meanings or intentions, but it's clear to see that body language, composition, and level of detail are definitely different.

In contrast to the celebration of classical civilisations in the nineteenth century, at the same time there was a phenomenon known as "Christian masculinity." There's a lot to unpack here. Christian masculinity was the idea that the meek, stoic, other-cheek-turning biblical message of Christianity wasn't setting a good example for the young men of the world because those were all seen as delicate, feminine virtues, and we don't want our boys to be sissies!

What they needed was a patriarchal society to show them that strength was godly, homosocial society wasn't depraved, power was a force for good, and fighting spirit was a method of spirituality. And then, as long as those men demonstrate their strength and power within our boundaries, under our control, and fight who we tell them to fight, they'll be a strong, healthy, Christian, and commanded army. None of that bourgeois Freedom, Beauty, Truth, and Love that Kylie Minogue's Green Fairy sings about in *Moulin Rouge!* In Eastern

Europe this particular brand of "a strong mind in a sound body" manifested in Sokols—gymnastics camps that included lectures and discussions, and physical, moral, and intellectual training. Fortunately for us, the marketing for Sokols ended up being some of the most camp Museum Bum imagery around (see page 135)!

Now that we're on to the twentieth century, let's talk about John Singer Sargent. The Sarg was a society portrait artist working in America and Europe. In 1918, the British Government commissioned him as a war artist to capture scenes of Americans and Brits in the First World War. Today the world generally understands that Sargent was living his life as a gay man, and that his most significant partner was Albert de Belleroche, but in Sarg's time, the phrase "lifelong bachelor" was how they decided to describe him. Have a look at *Tommies Bathing* by JSS on page 130. Not a bad life!

As you'll notice in this chapter, when it comes to bare-bottomed bathers, we see more white boys at the beach than anyone else. There are, however, a few notable exceptions to this general rule. We do see a few examples of women enjoying their time at the beach. What's more, we even see some women painting these scenes.

Dame Ethel Walker started painting at age thirty-eight. Although she was taught by artists who are still known today (like Walter Sickert, for one), she's not as well-known as she should be. She was once described as "England's leading woman artist," which prompted her to reply, "There's no such thing as a woman artist. There are only two kinds of artists—bad and good. You can call me a good artist if you like." We are going to call her a good

artist, and we're sure her 1920 piece *Decoration: The Excursion of Nausicaa* (page 145) will encourage you to agree. Walker, too, is inspired by the classical world and depicts a scene from Homer's *Odyssey*. She shows a princess and her attendants bathing themselves and washing their clothes in a river by the sea. The women working together offer a glimpse at a community in which everyone is helped and supported. It's an all-female utopia that offers a counterbalance to Tuke's all-male idyll.

Gerda Wegener's *A Summer Day* (page 89) is similar to Walker's piece; we see a group of women having a gay old time by the riverside. There's music and painting. There's flower-smelling and reading. The sunbeams are beating down on the group, adding to the hazy summer scene. It looks absolutely delightful. As with Walker's work, there's an interloper observing, but this time it's a woman who is looking at the group rather than a man, and this time, the interloper is noticed; her gaze is met and returned with an undeniable frisson by the accordion player. This is unusual. In our other beach scenes, the gaze, usually our own as viewers, is not returned. It's like we are at the beach, people watching. With Wegener we see the artist painting, and we are part of the picture and part of the action too, so it's only natural that we get to see things from a different perspective.

As we progress through the twentieth century, our waterfronts become more and more urbanised as city docks grow and more and more people want to live by the sea. Let's take a look at Edward Casey's *Stevedores Bathing under Brooklyn Bridge* (page 133) as an example of this waterfront overcrowding. Stevedores are people employed to load and unload ships at the docks. It would be hot, sweaty, and exhausting work, which is a lovely thematic link back to Duncan Grant (see the "Hella Good Bums and Heavenly Bottoms" chapter). A dip in the East River would be refreshing in theory, but with the ships chugging along in the water, a second thought might be wise. As with Tuke's work, it is thought that Casey would have painted his bathing dockers en plein air. To a casual observer on the shore at the time, Casey may have looked like an artist trying to capture the majesty of the Manhattan skyline. One look at his canvas clearly shows that his interest was not on the buildings.

New York in the 1930s was a melting pot of people and cultures in a way that rural Cornwall in the late 1800s to early 1900s never was. The dreamlike idyll of beach-bathing has become a respite from hard, backbreaking work. One thing that has stayed the same is the valuing of the muscular male form as an ideal of beauty. Even though Casey's cityscape is a wash of grey, his workers, like Tuke's frolicking swimmers, are bathed in golden sunlight.

Capturing images of pretty young things by the beach is not just confined to paintings. As cameras became more and more accessible and durable, we start to see more and more photographs of these subjects. Photography is a medium that can shine a light on the past in a way that paintings can't. By no means are cameras objective observers, because the person behind them is still trying to tell a story or capture the magic of a moment. There's a certain magic in *Young Man Posing for*

Polaroid (1959) (see page 127). Not only is the fashion incredible, but there is a playfulness in the photo. We can see a young man in a fetching cardigan posing for a picture, but the gentleman in the foreground with his back to us looks like he might be perfecting his posture too. This image is from Cherry Grove on Fire Island, a beach town just two hours away from busy and bustling NYC. The town was a favoured destination of New York theatrical types, and it became an early safe haven for LGBTQIA+ people. The Cherry Grove Archive, which looks after this image and plenty of other material, is a vital resource for LGBTQIA+ history in the USA.

Once you've finished this chapter, book a beach holiday. Don't pack swimming costumes but do pack a set of watercolours instead (and get consent!).

Thomas Eakins and John Laurie Wallace were professor and student at the Pennsylvania Academy of Fine Arts. In this c. 1883 image, part of the Met's photography collection, they're affecting the contrapposto poses of classical statues . . . for . . . *reads notes* . . . science . . .

I promise you, Charles, in sixty years the beach-cardigan combo will be everywhere!

In 2021, the New York Historical Society held a photography exhibition called "Safe/Haven: Gay Life in 1950s Cherry Grove," revealing the queer culture of the village on Fire Island, near New York City. *Young Man Posing for Polaroid*, 1959.

William-Adolphe Bouguereau with his unimagini-
tively titled *The Bathers*, 1884, on display at the Art
Institute of Chicago, USA. Just to prove that it's not
all boys.

After years of Zoom meetings can we please get back to the traditional meetings: naked in a group by a pond?
Paul Cézanne's *The Large Bathers*, 1900–1906, at the Philadelphia Museum of Art, USA.

John Singer Sargent's glorious *Man and Pool*, 1917, at the Met. Sargent used the labourers building his friends' garden in Miami as muscly models for his paintings.

This is one in a series John Singer Sargent was on government commission to paint of wartime Europe. *Tommies Bathing*, 1918, is on display at the Met in New York. Apparently, it was important to record two soldiers sneaking off for a bit of skinny-dipping and a nap together!

Thomas Eakins's *Swimming Hole*, 1885, from the Amon Carter Museum of American Art; and the photo study for the painting (from the Getty Center).

Choosing to imagine that all these groups are across the lake from each other, giggling and flirting and showing off across the water.

So wait, you're saying that your name is Steve Doors? I think you must have misunderstood the invitation, Steve.

Stevedores Bathing under Brooklyn Bridge by Edward Casey, 1939, was part of an exhibition by the Brooklyn Historical Society, "On the (Queer) Waterfront," at Brooklyn Public Library in 2019. The painting is owned by Green-Wood Cemetery in New York.

No look! I can only get the High G# if I clench!
    Thomas Eakins's *Thomas Eakins, Nude, Playing Pipes*, c. 1883, is part of the collection at the Met, New York.

SLET
SOKOLSTVA NA JADRANU
SPLIT ~ JUNI ~ 1931

Coming soon to a gym near you: moving rocks up a hill!

Really just want to go round making sure they've all got their sunscreen on.

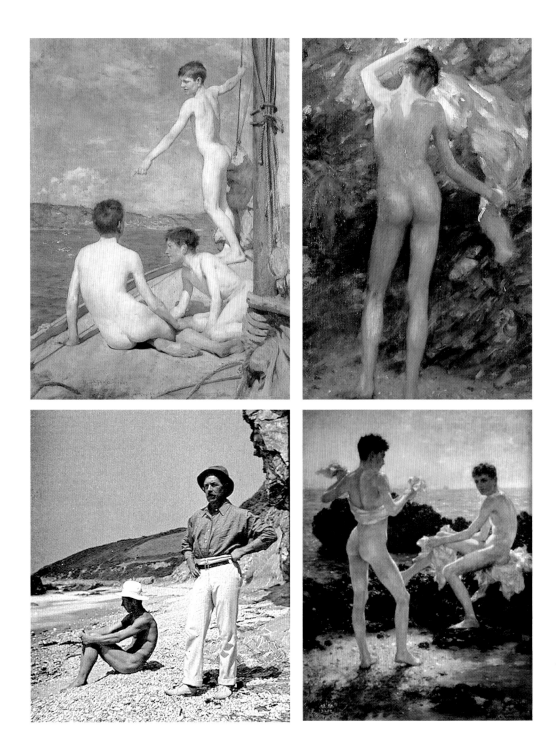

While in Cornwall, Tuke painted the locals, and while in Jamaica, he also painted the locals.

A lot of art is inpsired by other art. You can call it stealing or you can call it an homage. This feels like an artist recreating a favourite image in a different medium. Did artists unintentionally create meme culture?

Jeune homme nu assis au bord de la mer by Hippolyte Flandrin (below), 1836, at the Louvre, and *Caino* by Wilhelm von Gloeden (left), c. 1900, from Galerie Lampertz in Munich.

List's photography showing men, including Black men, stands in stark contrast to other fashion photographers of the 1930s, when the magazine zeitgeist was white women.

His work is undeniably sexy, but it didn't cross the line into controversy. Having said that, Herbert List's queer lens on photography inspired controversial superstar photographers Bruce Weber and Robert Mapplethorpe to push boundaries in the later twentieth century.

Armor II by Herbert List, 1934, "Herbert List Metamorphoses" exhibition in the Magnum Gallery in London in 2021.

Henrietta Skerrett Montalba's *Venetian Boy Catching a Crab* feels like he could teach the landscape gardener from John Singer Sargent's *Man and Pool* (page 129) a few lessons on crab-catching! We recommend using a net though, as crab pincers pack quite a punch.

Henrietta was the youngest of four artist-sisters, and she studied and worked in Venice and South Kensington, so it's very fitting that her most prominently featured work reflects both of these key places from her life.

The ancient version of your local craft group was a communal trip to the beach to have a wash and a chit chat. Dame Ethel Walker's Decoration: *The Excursion of Nausicaa*.

Herbert List definitely had a knack for a good photo! Beautiful statues enjoy being at the beach too. Antikythera statue went for a little dip in the sea a few thousand years ago and had to be excavated from the sea w millennia later.

THE
(REAR)
END

CREDITS

Cover image - *Venus and Mars*, 1793–1838, Angelo Bertini, after Giovanni Tognolli, after Antonio Canova. Photo by Rijksmuseum. Licensed under CC0.

P6 - *Dancing Sailors*, 1917, Charles Demuth. Photo by Cleveland Museum of Art. Licensed under CC0.

[All] Women Are from Venus (?)

P10 - *Venus and Adonis*, 1550s, Titian. Metropolitan Museum of Art. Licensed under CC0.

P15 - *Venus de Milo*, 150–125 BCE, Alexandros of Antioch. Musée du Louvre. Licensed under CC0.

P16 - *Venus Callipyge*, 1952, David Seymour. Magnum Images. Reproduced with permission.

P17 - *Venus Callipyge*, c. 100 BCE, unknown artist. Photo by Berthold Werner, Naples National Archaeological Museum. Licensed under CC3.0.

P17 - *Aphrodite of Knidos* (cast), 350 BCE (original), unknown artist. Photo by Zde, Gallery of Classical Art, Hostinné. Licensed under CC4.0.

P18 - *Venus del espejo (The Rokeby Venus)*, 1647–1651, Diego Velázquez. The National Gallery (UK). Licensed under CC0.

P18 - *Photograph of Mary Raleigh Richardson taken by a Scotland Yard detective*. c. 1913, Scotland Yard. Licensed under CC0.

P18 - *Detail from a photo (before the repairs) showing damage done to Rokeby Venus by Mary Richardson*, 1914. Photo by the National Gallery (UK). Licensed under CC0.

P19 - *Venus of Willendorf*, 2300–2800 BCE. Photo by Thirunavukkarasye-Raveendran, Natural History Museum, Vienna, Austria. Licensed under CC0.

P19 - *Gonnersdorf Venuses*, 2006, unknown artist. Photo by Gaudzinski-Windheuser and Jöris, Landesmuseum, Bonn, Germany. Licensed under CC4.0.

P20 - *Vestonicka venuse back*, 2007, unknown artist. Photo by Petr Novák, the National Museum, Prague. Licensed under CC2.5.

P20 - *Venus of Lespugue*, 2018, unknown artist. Photo by Vassil, Musée de l'Homme, Paris. Licensed under CC0.

P20 - *Replica of the Venus of Lespugue*, 2006. Digital image by José-Manuel Benito, Musée de l'Homme, Paris. Licensed under CC0.

P21 - *The Birth of Venus*, c. 1516, Marco Dente, after Raphael. Digitisation by Cleveland Museum of Art. Licensed under CC0.

P22 - *Vénus de Monruz*, 2014 (photo), unknown artist. Digital Image by Archives Laténium Neuchâtel. Licensed under CC4.0.

P22 - *Kostenki I Venus*, 2019 (photo), unknown artist. Photo by Don Hitchcock, Hermitage Museum, Russia. Licensed under CC4.0.

P23 - *Marble female figure*, 4500–4000 BCE, unknown artist. Photo by the Metropolitan Museum of Art. Licensed under CC0.

P24 - *Venus and Mars*, 1793–1838, Angelo Bertini, after Giovanni Tognolli, after Antonio Canova. Digitised by Rijksmuseum. Licensed under CC0.

P25 - *Venus*, 1790–1844, Domenico Marchetti, after Giovanni Tognolli, after Antonio Canova. Digitised by Rijksmuseum. Licensed under CC0.

P26 - *Back view of Venus reclining accompanied by Cupid with a harp, from "Oeuvre de Canova: Recueil de Statues . . ."* 1817, Domenico Marchetti. Digitised by the Metropolitan Museum of Art. Licensed under CC0.

P27 - *Venus of the Rags*, 1967, Michelangelo Pistoletto. Photo by Tate. Reproduced with permission from Cittadellarte.

Gods and Monsters

P28 - *The Perseus Series - Doom Fulfilled*, 1900 (published), Sir Edward Burne-Jones. Image digitisation by Birmingham Museums Trust. Licensed under CC0.

P30 - *Vulcan*, 2011 (photo), Giuseppe Moretti. Photo by Greg Willis. Licensed under CC2.0.

P34 - *Pan and Psyche*, 1900 (published), Sir Edward Burne-Jones. Image digitisation by Birmingham Museums Trust. Licensed under CC0.

P35 - *Antinous Farnese*, c. 100, unknown artist. Photo by Marie-Lan Nguyen. Licensed under CC2.5.

P35 - *Hercules and Antaeus*, 1877, Eugène Lacomblé. Photo by Rijksmuseum. Licensed under CC0.

P35 - *Apollo and Marsyas*, 1611–1623, Pieter Feddes van Harlingen. Photo by Rijksmuseum. Licensed under CC0.

P36 - *Marble Statue Group of the Three Graces*, c. 200, unknown artist. Photo by the Metropolitan Museum of Art. Licensed under CC0.

P37 - *Paris*, in or after 1785, Angelo Testa, Giovanni Tognolli, Antonio Canova. Photo by the Rijksmuseum. Licensed under CC0.

P38 - *Pluto*, 1588–1590, Hendrick Goltzius. Image digitised by the Rijksmuseum. Licensed under CC0.

P39 - *Hercules in gevecht met Cerberus*, c. 1500–1599, Monogrammist FP (Italië; 16e eeuw). Image digitised by the Rijksmuseum. Licensed under CC0.

P39 - *The Intoxication of Wine*, c. 1780–1790, Clodion (Claude Michel). Digitised by the Metropolitan Museum of Art. Licensed under CC0.

P40 - *Nymphaeum*, 1878, William-Adolphe Bouguereau. Image digitised by Haggin Museum, Stockton, CA. Licensed under CC0.

P54 - *The Hermaphrodite*, c. 1861 (photograph), Robert MacPherson (photographer). Digitisation by the Metropolitan Museum of Art. Licensed under CC0.

P54 - *Photograph of tattooed back. Psyche and Amour. (Captain Studdy)*, 1905, Sutherland Macdonald. The National Archives (UK). Reproduced with permission.

P54 - *The Sirens*, 1878–1880, Sir Edward Burne-Jones. Digital Image by Birmingham Museum and Art Gallery. Licensed under CC0.

P55 - *Hylas and the Nymphs, a Gallo-Roman mosaic*, c. 300 CE. Photo by Vassil. Licensed under CC0.

P55 - *Adam en Eva*, 1529, Anton von Woensam (and anonymous printmaker). Digital image by Rijksmuseum. Licensed under CC0.

P56 - *The Fisherman and the Syren*, 1856–1858, Frederic Leighton. Photo from Bridgeman Images, © Bristol Museums, Galleries & Archives/Given by Mrs. Charles Lyell, 1938. Reproduced with permission.

P57 - *Theseus and the Minotaur*, 1936. Herbert List. Tuileries Gardens, Paris. © Herbert List/Magnum Photos. Reproduced with permission.

P57 - *Legs of Hermes*, 1937, Herbert List. Chalcis, Greece. © Herbert List/Magnum Photos. Reproduced with permission.

P58 - *Archetypal Media Image: Classical*, 1977, Hal Fischer (Gay Semiotics). © 2022. Digital image by the Museum of Modern Art, New York/Scala, Florence.

P59 - *Adam*, c. 1490–1495, Tullio Lombardo. Photo by the Metropolitan Museum of Art. Licensed under CC0.

Hella Good Bums and Heavenly Bottoms

PP60–61 - *The Garden of Earthly Delights*, c. 1495–1505, Hieronymus Bosch. Photo by Museo del Prado. Licensed under CC0.

P62 - *Mural in the Russell Chantry*, 1953, Duncan Grant. Photo by Andy Scott. Licensed under CC4.0.

P64 - *The Crucifixion and The Last Judgment (detail)*, c. 1430–1440, Jan van Eyck. Photo by Metropolitan Museum of Art. Licensed under CC0.

P65 - *Le Génie du Mal*, 1842 (installation), Joseph Geefs. Photo by C. Verhelst, Royal Museums of Fine Arts of Belgium, Brussels, inv. 1558. Reproduced with permission.

P65 - *Statue of Lucifer in Liège Cathedral*, 2013 (photo). Liége Cathedral. Photo by Jeran Renz. Licensed under CC3.0.

P68 - *Carved misericord in the stalls*, 1784–1824. Hugh O'Neill. Bristol Museum and Art Gallery, UK. © Bristol Museums, Galleries & Archives/Bequest of William Jerdone Braikenridge, 1908/Bridgeman Images. Reproduced with permission.

P68 - *A Misericord depicting "The Romance of Reynard the Fox,"* 1520. Bristol Museum and Art Gallery, UK. © Bristol Museums, Galleries & Archives/Bridgeman Images. Reproduced with permission.

P69 - *Oude Kerke misericord*, 2010 (photo). Photo by Murgatroyd49, Oude Kerk, Amsterdam. Licensed under CC4.0.

P69 - *Carving depicting a coppersmith, from a choir stall, fifteenth century, French School*, fifteenth century. Musee National du Moyen Age et des Thermes de Cluny, Paris/Bridgeman Images. Reproduced with permission.

P70 - *Boston Stump Misericord 03*, 25 July 2006 (photo). Photo by Immanuel Giel, Boston Stump Church, Lincolnshire, UK. Licensed under public domain.

P70 - *The All Saints Halifax Man*, 2022 (photo). Photo by Reverend Jae Chandler, All Saints Church, Hereford. Reproduced with permission.

PP71–73 (all images) - *The Garden of Earthly Delights*, c. 1495–1505, Hieronymus Bosch. Photo by Museo del Prado. Licensed under CC0.

P74 - *The Garden of Earthly Delights*, c. 1495–1505, Hieronymus Bosch. Photo by Museo del Prado. Licensed under CC0.

P74 - *Butt Song*, c. 2020, ChaosControlled123/Amelie. Digital Image by Greg Harradine. Reproduced with permission.

P75 - *Untitled*, 1990, Robert Gober. Matthew Marks Gallery. Reproduced with permission.

P76 - *Cain and Abel (?)*, seventeenth century, Netherlandish. Photo by Metropolitan Museum of Art. Licensed under CC0.

P77 - *Cain murdering Abel (plate 2 from The Story of Cain and Abel)*, 1576, Johann Sadeler I. Digital image by the Metropolitan Museum of Art. Licensed under CC0.

P77 - *Cain and Abel*, 1910, Svend Rathsack. Photo by Chaumot. Licensed under CC0.

PP78–79 (all images) - *Last Judgement*, c. 1526, Lucas van Leyden. Photo by Museum De Lakenhal/Rijksmuseum. Licensed under CC0.

P80 - *Lucifer*, c. 1950 (photo), Jacob Epstein (sculptor). Photo by Birmingham Museums Trust. Licensed under CC0.

P81 - *Angel of the North*, 2011 (photo), Antony Gormley. Photo by Barly. Licensed under CC2.0.

P81 - *Study for "St George slaying the Dragon,"* 1685–1686, Sir Edward Burne-Jones. Digital Image by Birmingham Museums Trust. Licensed under CC0.

P82 - *The Archangel Michael Fighting the Rebel Angels*, 1621, Lucas Vorsterman (I), after Peter Paul Rubens. Digital image by Rijksmuseum. Licensed under CC0.

P83 - *Caron passant les ombres*, c. 1735, Pierre Subleyras. Photo by Musée du Louvre/Scala Images. Reproduced with permission.

P84 - *Orpheus*, 1916, Charles H. Niehaus. Photo by Vespasian/Alamy Stock Photo. Reproduced with permission.

P85 - *Satan Arousing the Rebel Angels*, 1808, William Blake. Digital image by the V&A (2006AU5677). Reproduced with permission.

P85 - *Witches Going to Their Sabbath*, 1878, Luis Ricardo Falero. Photo by www.artrenewal.org. Licensed under CC0.

P85 - *The Witch*, 1882, Luis Ricardo Falero. Photo by Talabardon & Gautier. Licensed under CC0.

They're Just Good Friends

PP86–87 - *Dancing Sailors*, 1917, Charles Demuth. Photo by Cleveland Museum of Art. Licensed under CC0.

P89 - *A Summer Day*, 1927, Gerda Wegener. Photo by Kruusamägi, exhibited at Arken Museum of Modern Art, 2015–2016. Licensed under CC0.

P91 - *Achilles Removing Patroclus's Body from the Battle*, c. 1547, Léon Davent. Digitisation by the Metropolitan Museum of Art in New York. Licensed under CC0.

P91 - *Achilles Sacrificing His Hair on the Funeral Pyre of Patroclus*, 1795–1800, Henry Fuseli. In Frederick Antal's, *Estudios sobre Fuseli,* Madrid: Visor, 1989. ISBN 84-7774-510-2. Licensed under CC0.

P91 - *Crop from "Polyphemus and Galatea, with Apollo and Hyacinthus above,"* c. 1670, P. Aquila. Wellcome Collection. Licensed under CC4.0.

P92 - *Crop from "In het Atrium is plaats voor beelden uit de collectie,"* 2013. Photo by Rijksvastgoedbedrijf, Rijksmuseum, Amsterdam, Netherlands. Licensed under public domain.

P92 - *Harmodius and Aristogeiton*, 2017 (photo). Photo by Miguel Hermoso Cuesta, exhibited at National Archaeological Museum of Naples. Licensed under CC4.0.

P93 - *Battle of the Nudes*, c. 1470–1480, Antonio del Pollaiuolo. Digital image by Cleveland Museum of Art. Licensed under CC0.

P93 - *Hercules verslaat de Hydra van Lerna*, 1545, Hans Sebald Beham. Digital image by Rijksmuseum. Licensed under CC0.

P94 - *Red-figured kylix "Zephyr and Hyacinth,"* 490–485 BCE, Duris. Photo by Boston Museum of Fine Arts. Licensed under CC0.

P95 - *Nisus and Euryalus*, 1607–1612, Jean-Baptiste-Louis Roman. On display at Musée du Louvre. Inv.: MR303; Photographer: Mathieu Rabeau © 2022. RMN-Grand Palais/Dist. Photo Scala, Florence. Reproduced with permission.

P96 - *Orpheus*, 1896, John Macallan Swan. Digital image by Lady Lever Art Gallery. Licensed under CC0.

P96 - *Orpheus*, 1600–1601, Cristofano da Bracciano. Photo by Yair Haklai, Metropolitan Museum of Art. Licensed under CC4.0.

P97 - *Untitled (Three Nude Figures),* date unknown, Alvin Baltrop. Exhibited at Exile Gallery, Vienna, Austria, 2015. © ARS, New York and DACS, London 2022. Reproduced with permission.

P97 - *The Bath*, 1951. Paul Cadmus. Digital image by Whitney Museum of American Art. Licensed by Scala.

P98 - *Finistere*, 1952, Paul Cadmus. Digital image by Whitney Museum of American Art. Licensed by Scala. Reproduced with permission.

P98 - *The Penitent and Impenitent Thieves*, 1611, Abraham Janssens. Photo by Daderot. Museum de Fundatie, Zwolle, Netherlands. Reproduced with permission.

P99 - *Wrestlers*, c. 1700s, unknown artist. Photo by Daderot, Accademia Ligustica di Belle Arti (copy of the Roman version in the Uffizi Gallery). Licensed under CC1.0.

P100 - *Antieke steen*, 1776–1851, Daniël Veelwaard (printmaker), after Pierre Lacour (artist). Image digitisation by Rijksmuseum. Licensed under CC0.

P100 - *Wrestling Match*, 1649, Michiel Sweerts. Staatliche Kunsthalle Karlsruhe, Germany. Licensed under CC0.

P100 - *Ganymede and the Eagle*, 1921, John Singer Sargent. Boston Museum of Fine Arts. Licensed under CC0.

P101 - *Signifiers for a Male Response from the series "Gay Semiotics,"* 1977, Hal Fischer. Geraldine Murphy Fund. Museum of Modern Art (MoMA), New York. Accession no: 714.2017.1. © 2022. Digital image, The Museum of Modern Art, New York/Scala, Florence. Reproduced with permission.

When Is a Bum Not a Bum?

P102 - *Four Apricots on a Stone Plinth*, 1698, Adriaen Coorte. Rijksmuseum. Licensed under CC0.

P104 - *Honey-Pop Armchair*, 2000, Tokujin Yoshioka. Museum of Modern Art (MoMA), New York. Accession no: 262.2002.1-2. © 2022. Digital image, The Museum of Modern Art, New York/Scala, Florence. Reproduced with permission.

P105 - *Frescos of three vignettes of fruit*, 45–79 CE, unknown artist. Digital image by Andrew Dalby, Casa dei Cervi, Herculaneum; National Archaeological Museum of Naples. Licensed under CC0.

P107 - *Large Two Forms* (LH 556), 1966, Henry Moore. The Henry Moore Foundation. Reproduced by permission of the Henry Moore Foundation.

P108 - *Cartoon Museum Benches*, 2005 (gifted to Cartoon Museum by the Museum of London after the "Art of Satire" exhibition). Photos by Holly T. Burrows. (Print is a crop from *The Graces in a High Wind*, 1810, James Gillray. The British Museum. Reproduced with permission.)

P109 - *Vase* (image 2006AW2181), 1968, Hans Coper. © Jane Coper and the estate of the artists/Victoria and Albert Museum. On display at the Victoria and Albert Museum, London, UK. Reproduced with permission.

P110 - *Amethyst Bull's-Head Amulet*, c. 3500–2950 BCE, unknown artist. Cleveland Museum of Art. Licensed under CC0.

P110 - *Museum of the Moon*, 2016, Luke Jerram. Photo by Mark Small. Reproduced with permission.

P111 - *Three Peaches on a Stone Plinth*, 1705, Adriaen Coorte. Digital image by Rijksmuseum. Licensed under CC0.

P112 - *Portions of a Costume Armor*, c. 1525, Kolman Helmschmid. Photo by The Metropolitan Museum of Art. Licensed under CC0.

P113 - *Le Violon d'Ingres*, 1924, Man Ray. © DACS, London/The Man Ray Trust. Reproduced with permission.

P114 - *Etude de Rhythm*, 1910, John Duncan Fergusson. The Fergusson Gallery, Culture Perth and Kinross, Scotland. © Perth & Kinross Council/Bridgeman Images. Reproduced with permission.

P115 - *Adidas Team GB swimming trunks used by Tom Daley*, 2012, Stella McCartney; Adidas; British Olympic Association. Museum of London (reference number: 2012.83). Reproduced with permission.

P116 - *Black Loch Bowl*, discovered in 2018, artist unknown. Photo by AOC Archaeology, Black Loch of Myrton, Dumfries and Galloway Museums/Historic Environment Scotland. Reproduced with permission.

P116 - *Black Loch Bowl: reconstruction*, c. 2018, Dumfries and Galloway Museums/Historic Environment Scotland. Reproduced with permission.

P117 - *Vase*, 1913, Taxile Doat. Saint Louis Art Museum, USA. Licensed under CC0.

P118 - *Soldiers at Rye*, 1941, Edward Burra. Tate, London. Reproduced with permission.

P118 - *Female fruit Lodoicea maldivica*, 2010. Photo by Brocken Inaglory. Licensed under CC0.

P119 - *A Naked Visit to the Royal Academy of Arts*, 2019. Photo by Tristan Fewings, © Getty Images. Reproduced with permission.

Beach Bums

PP120–121 - *Seven Bathers*, 1900, Paul Cézanne. Beyeler Foundation. Licensed under CC0.

P126 - *[Thomas Eakins and John Laurie Wallace on a Beach]*, c. 1883, unknown photographer. Metropolitan Museum of Art, New York. Licensed under CC0.

P127 - *Young man posing for Polaroid in Cherry Grove, Fire Island*, 1959, unknown photographer. Cherry Grove Archives Collection, exhibited at "Safe/Haven: Gay Life in 1950s Cherry Grove," New York Historical Society, 2021. Reproduced with permission.

P128 - *The Bathers*, 1884, William-Adolphe Bouguereau. Art Institute Chicago, USA. Licensed under CC0.

P129 - *Les Grandes Baigneuses*, 1906, Paul Cézanne. Photo by Philadelphia Museum of Art. Licensed under CC0.

P129 - *Man and Pool*, Florida, 1917, John Singer Sargent. Metropolitan Museum of Art. © The Metropolitan Museum of Art/Art Resource/Scala, Florence. Reproduced with permission.

P130 - *Tommies Bathing*, 1918, John Singer Sargent. Photo by The Metropolitan Museum of Art. Licensed under CC1.0.

P131 - *Swimming / The Swimming Hole*, 1885, Thomas Eakins. Photo by Amon Carter Museum of American Art. Licensed under CC0.

P131 - *Eakins's Students at the "The Swimming Hole,"* 1884, Thomas Eakins. Getty Center. Licensed under CC0.

P132 - *Baigneuses*, 1902–1906, Paul Cézanne. Private Collection. Licensed under CC0.

P132 - *The Bathers*, 1897, Paul Cézanne. Cleveland Museum of Art. Licensed under CC0.

P132 - *Bathers*, 1890–1892, Paul Cézanne. Saint Louis Art Museum. Licensed under CC0.

P133 - *Stevedores Bathing under Brooklyn Bridge*, 1939, Edward Casey. © Green-Wood Cemetery. Reproduced with permission.

P134 - *[Thomas Eakins, Nude, Playing Pipes]*, c. 1883, unknown photographer. Metropolitan Museum of Art, USA. Licensed under CC0.

P135 - *1931 Sokol Society Event on the Adriatic Coast (Slet Sokolstua Na Jadranu Split - Juni - 1931)*, 1931, unknown artist. Muzej Grada Splita. Reproduced with permission.

P136 - *Boy on a beach*, 1912, Henry Scott Tuke. Digital image by easyart.com. Licensed under CC0.

P136 - *A standing male nude*, 1914, Henry Scott Tuke. Digital image by Christie's. Licensed under CC0.

P136 - *A Holiday*, 1921. Henry Scott Tuke. Trinity College Cambridge. Digital image by Christie's. Licensed under CC0.

P136 - *A Bathing Group*, 1914, Henry Scott Tuke. Royal Academy of Arts. Licensed under CC0.

P137 - *July Sun*, 1913, Henry Scott Tuke. Royal Academy of Arts. Licensed under CC0.

P137 - *Midsummer Morning (Lovers of the Sun)*, 1908, Henry Scott Tuke. Exhibited in the Royal Academy, London, 1908. Licensed under CC0.

P137 - *Gleaming Waters*, 1910, Henry Scott Tuke. Digital image by Christie's. Licensed under CC0.

P137 - *Lovers of the Sun*, 1923, Henry Scott Tuke. Photo by G.dallorto, exhibited at the Royal Academy in London, 1908. Licensed under CC0.

P138 - *The Bather*, 1924, Henry Scott Tuke. Digital image by Christie's. Licensed under CC0.

P139 - *Ruby, Gold and Malachite*, 1902, Henry Scott Tuke. Guildhall Art Gallery, London. Licensed under CC0.

P139 - *The three companions*, 1905, Henry Scott Tuke. Digital image by G.dallorto. Licensed under CC0.

P139 - *A Bathing Group*, 1912, Henry Scott Tuke. Falmouth Art Gallery, UK. Licensed under CC0.

P140 - *The Bathers*, 1889, Henry Scott Tuke. Leeds Art Gallery, UK. Licensed under CC0.

P140 - *The Blue Jacket*, 1918, Henry Scott Tuke. Kirklees Museums and Galleries, UK. Licensed under CC0.

MUSEUM BUMS: FURTHER READING
(More about that Bass)

If this book has left you desperate to dive deeper into the world of bottoms, butts, and bums in art, here are some more books to help you on your way.

Barlow, Clare, ed., *Queer British Art: 1861–1867*. London: Tate Publishing, 2017.

Berger, John. *Ways of Seeing*. 1972. New York: Penguin Random House, 2008.

Clarke, Kenneth. *Civilisation*. London: John Murray, 2018.

Ellis, Martin, Timothy Barringer, and Victoria Osborne. *Victorian Radicals: From the Pre-Raphaelites to the Arts and Crafts Movement*. New York: American Federation of Arts, 2018.

Field, D. M. *The Nude in Art*. London: WH Smith, 1981.

Jenkins, Ian. *Defining Beauty: The Body in Ancient Greek Art*. London: British Museum Press, 2015.

Millington, Ruth. *Muse*. London: Square Peg, 2022.

Ovid. *Metamorphoses*. Oxford University Press, 1998.

Parkinson, R. B. *A Little Gay History*. London: British Museum Press, 2013.

Pilcher, Alex. *A Queer Little History of Art*. London: Tate Publishing, 2017.

Robinson, Cicely, ed., *Henry Scott Tuke*. London: Yale University Press, 2021.

Simblet, Sarah. *Anatomy for the Artist*. London: DK, 2001.

The Metropolitan Museum of Art Guide. New York: Metropolitan Museum of Art, 2019. Distributed by Yale University Press.

Woodford, Susan. *An Introduction to Greek Art*. 1986. London: Duckworth, 1997.

@MuseumBums: Breaking the Internet

A new bum is shared daily on @MuseumBums on social media, and there is even more
butt-tastic content on the website www.museumbums.com.

ACKNOWLEDGEMENTS

As you can imagine, we spend a lot of time ruminating about butts, bottoms, rear ends, and derrieres. We would like to thank all the people involved in turning our thoughts into the very book you're holding in your hands.

There wouldn't be a book at all without Glen Weldon and his podcast *Pop Culture Happy Hour*, which put us on the radar of our incredible agent, Maggie Cooper. She has held our hands right from the "hey, this a book" stage all the way to "omg—it's on the shelves!" Maggie has made this often-daunting process a dream come true, and we cannot thank her enough.

Thanks also goes to Dylan Glynn, who generously worked on a lot of the preliminary design for our pitch, and to Susanne Turner, the curator at Cambridge's Museum of Classical Archaeology, who bravely let us loose in her museum to point at and count all the butts she has on display. Clearly everything worked out as we were able to verify that she has the most butts on display out of any museum in the UK.

Our friends Imogen, Helen, Robert, and Powder have stuck by us while we dragged them on bum-hunting expeditions and messaged them sneak peeks at every step of the process. Our family is very proud that we've written a book, but we think they might be a little confused about the subject.

At Chronicle we're forever grateful to our editors, Becca Hunt and Olivia Roberts, who developed our stack of ideas and terrible bum puns into an actual, real-life book. We are still pinching ourselves (it can't be real, can it?). Maggie "Maggie the Designer" Edelman transformed our spreadsheets and image folders into the jaw-dropping beauty that you've just read; the work of a true artist! We're ever grateful to the whole team at Chronicle in the US and Abrams & Chronicle in the UK for seeing the potential in us and our ideas.

We'd also like to thank everyone who's ever followed our Twitter and Instagram, liked one of our posts, commented on them, or sent us a photo of a Museum Bum to be shared.